STAR WARS®

CLONE WARS

ADVENTURES

VOLUME 4

designers
Darin Fabrick and Joshua Elliott

assistant editor
Dave Marshall

editor
Jeremy Barlow

publisher
Mike Richardson

special thanks to Sue Rostoni, Leland Chee, and Amy Gary at
Lucas Licensing

talk about this book online at: *www.darkhorse.com/community/boards*

The events in this story take place
just before and during the events in
Star Wars: Episode III *Revenge of the Sith*

Advertising Sales: (503) 652-8815 x370
Comic Shop Locator Service: (888) 266-4226
darkhorse.com
starwars.com

3 5 7 9 10 8 6 4

STAR WARS: CLONE WARS ADVENTURES Volume 4, September 2005. Published by Dark
Horse Books, a division of Dark Horse Comics, Inc., 10956 SE Main Street, Milwaukie, OR 97222.
Star Wars ©2005 Lucasfilm Ltd. & ™. All rights reserved. Used under authorization. Text and
illustrations for Star Wars are © 2005 Lucasfilm Ltd. Dark Horse Books™ is a trademark of Dark
Horse Comics, Inc. All rights reserved. No portion of this publication may be reproduced or
transmitted, in any form or by any means, without the express written permission of Dark Horse
Comics, Inc. Names, characters, places, and incidents featured in this publication either are the
product of the author's imagination or are used fictitiously. Any resemblance to actual persons
(living or dead), events, institutions, or locales, without satiric intent, is coincidental.
PRINTED IN CHINA

CLONE WARS

ADVENTURES

VOLUME 4

"ANOTHER FINE MESS"
script and art The Fillbach Brothers
colors Pamela Rambo

"THE BRINK"
script Justin Lambros
art The Fillbach Brothers
colors Dan Jackson

"ORDERS"
script Ryan Kaufman
art Rick Lacy
colors Ronda Pattison

"DESCENT"
script Haden Blackman
art The Fillbach Brothers
colors Dave Nestelle

lettering
Michael David Thomas

cover
The Fillbach Brothers and Dan Jackson

Dark Horse Books™

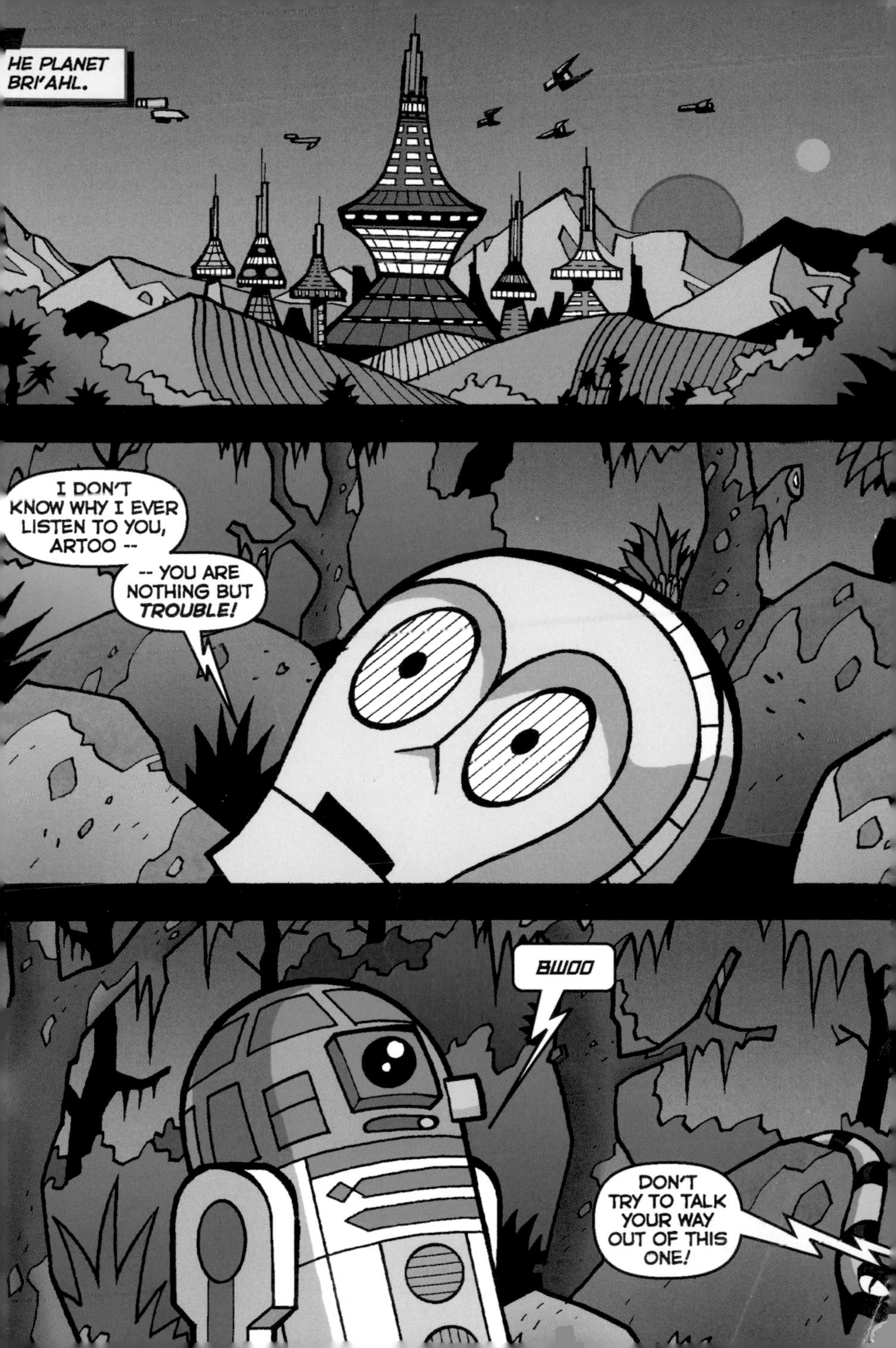
HE PLANET BRI'AHL.
I DON'T KNOW WHY I EVER LISTEN TO YOU, ARTOO --
-- YOU ARE NOTHING BUT *TROUBLE!*
BWOO
DON'T TRY TO TALK YOUR WAY OUT OF THIS ONE!

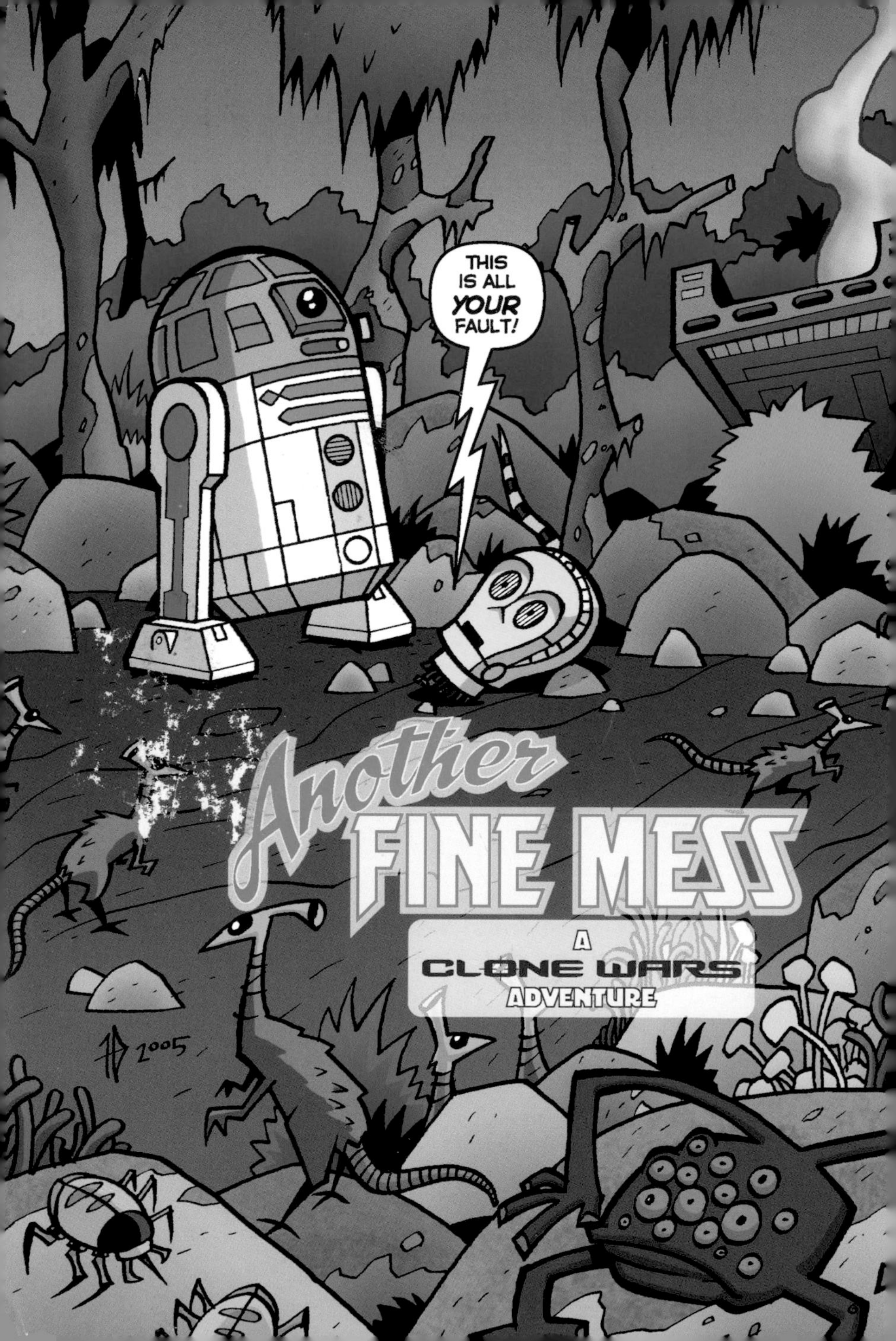
THIS IS ALL YOUR FAULT!
Another FINE MESS
A CLONE WARS ADVENTURE

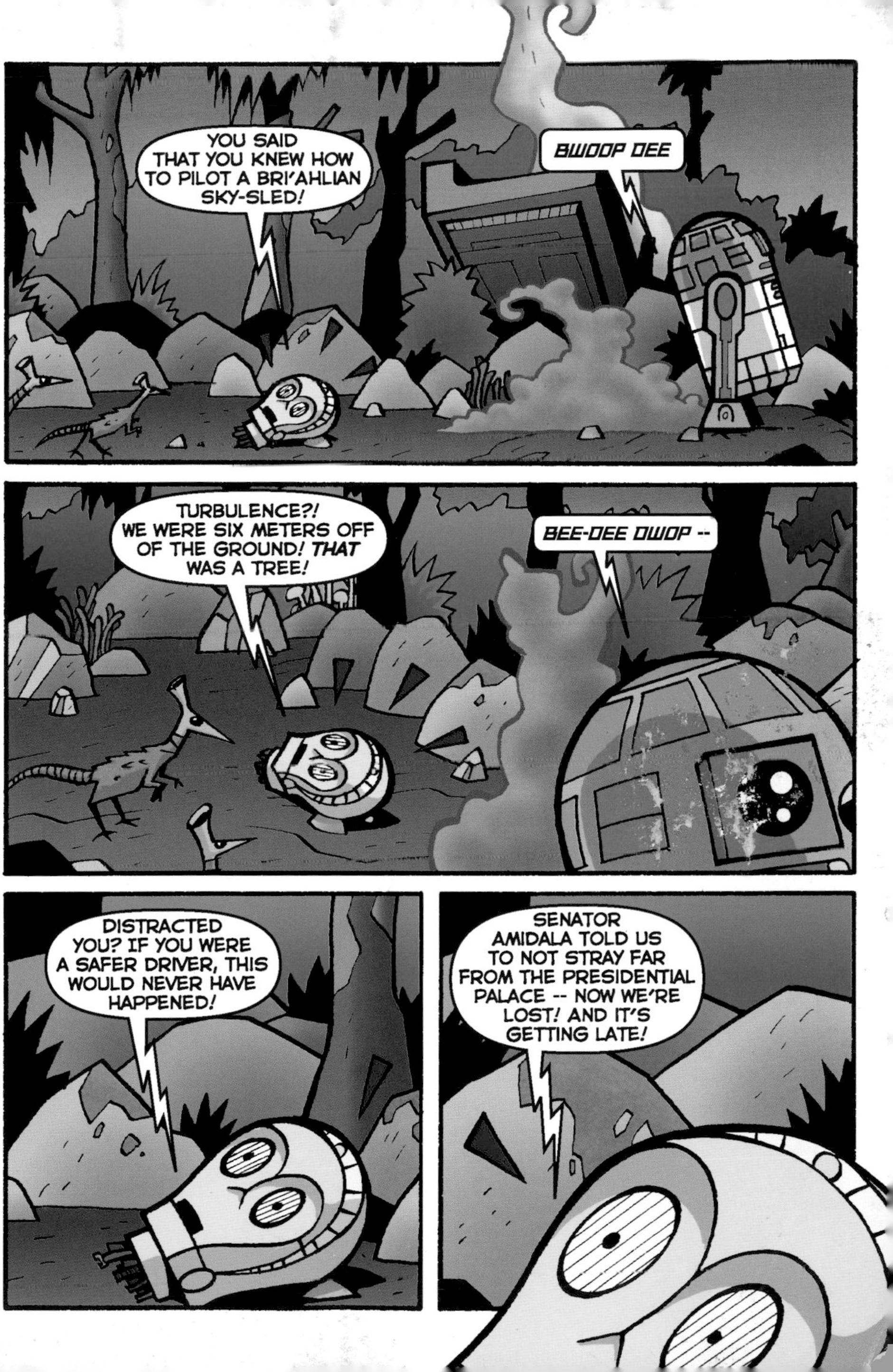
YOU SAID THAT YOU KNEW HOW TO PILOT A BRI'AHLIAN SKY-SLED!
BWOOP DEE
TURBULENCE?! WE WERE SIX METERS OFF OF THE GROUND! *THAT* WAS A TREE!
BEE-DEE DWOP --
DISTRACTED YOU? IF YOU WERE A SAFER DRIVER, THIS WOULD NEVER HAVE HAPPENED!
SENATOR AMIDALA TOLD US TO NOT STRAY FAR FROM THE PRESIDENTIAL PALACE -- NOW WE'RE LOST! AND IT'S GETTING LATE!

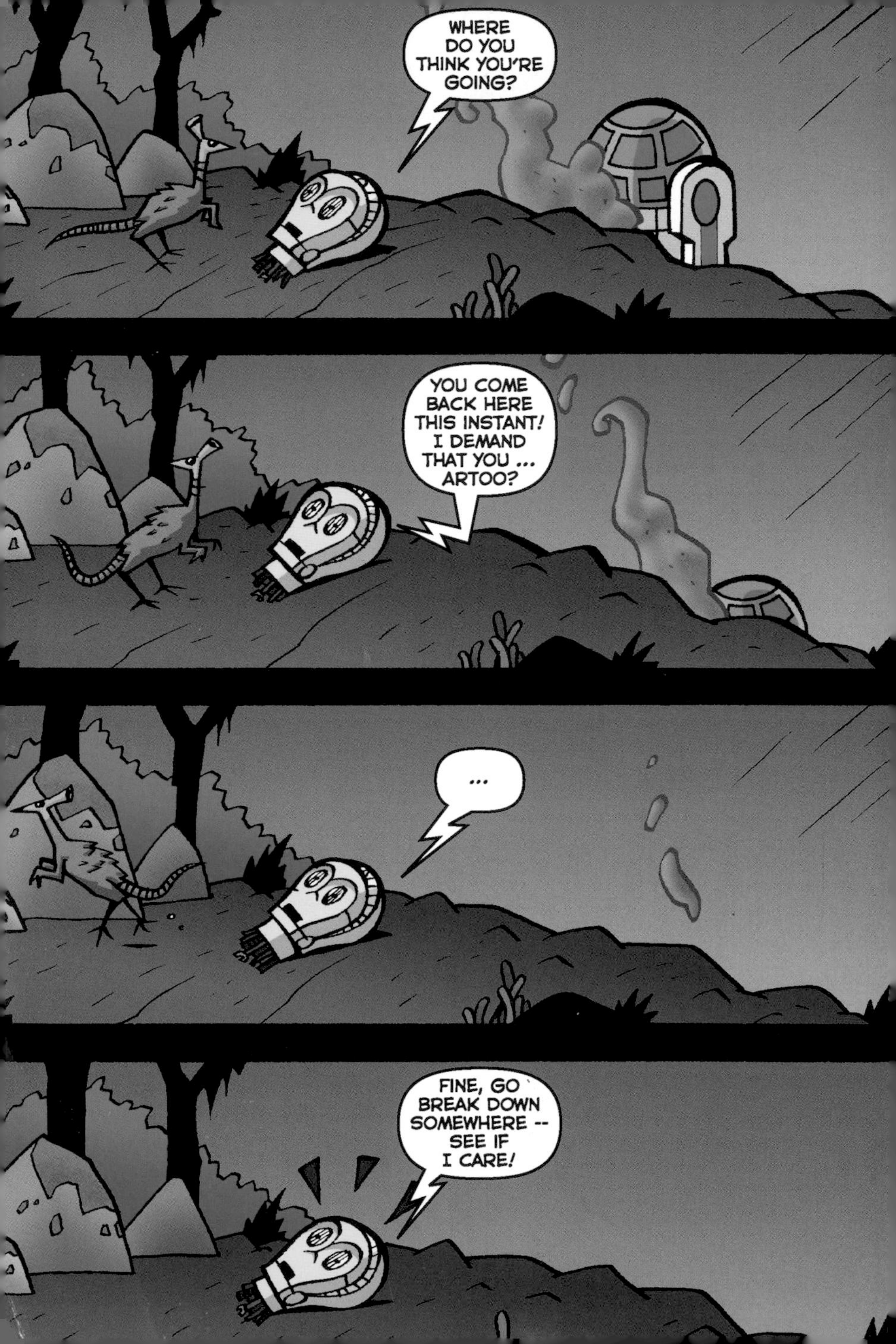
WHERE DO YOU THINK YOU'RE GOING?
YOU COME BACK HERE THIS INSTANT! I DEMAND THAT YOU ... ARTOO?
...
FINE, GO BREAK DOWN SOMEWHERE -- SEE IF I CARE!

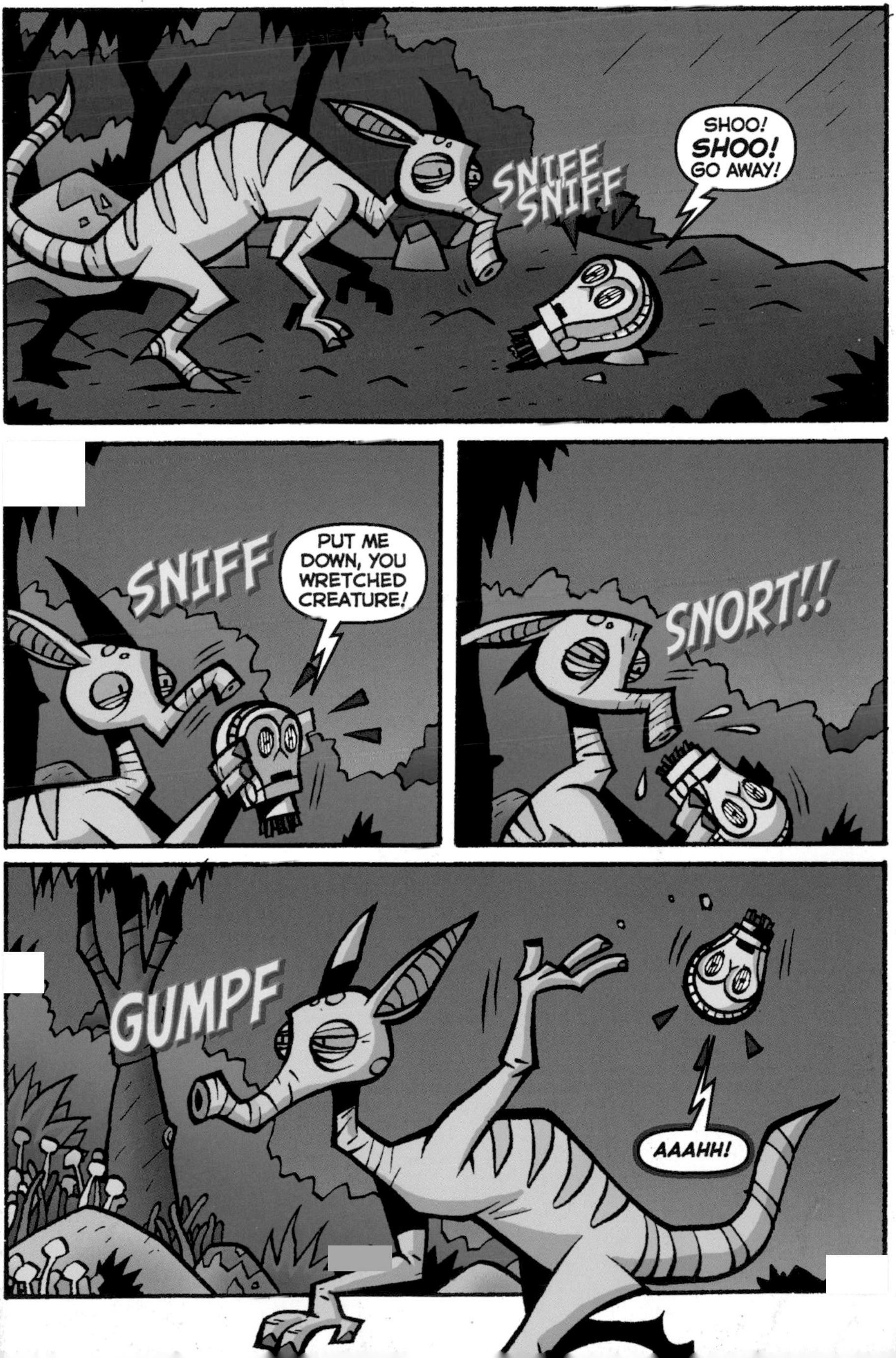
SNIFF SNIFF
SHOO! SHOO! GO AWAY!
SNIFF
PUT ME DOWN, YOU WRETCHED CREATURE!
SNORT!!
GUMPF
AAAHH!

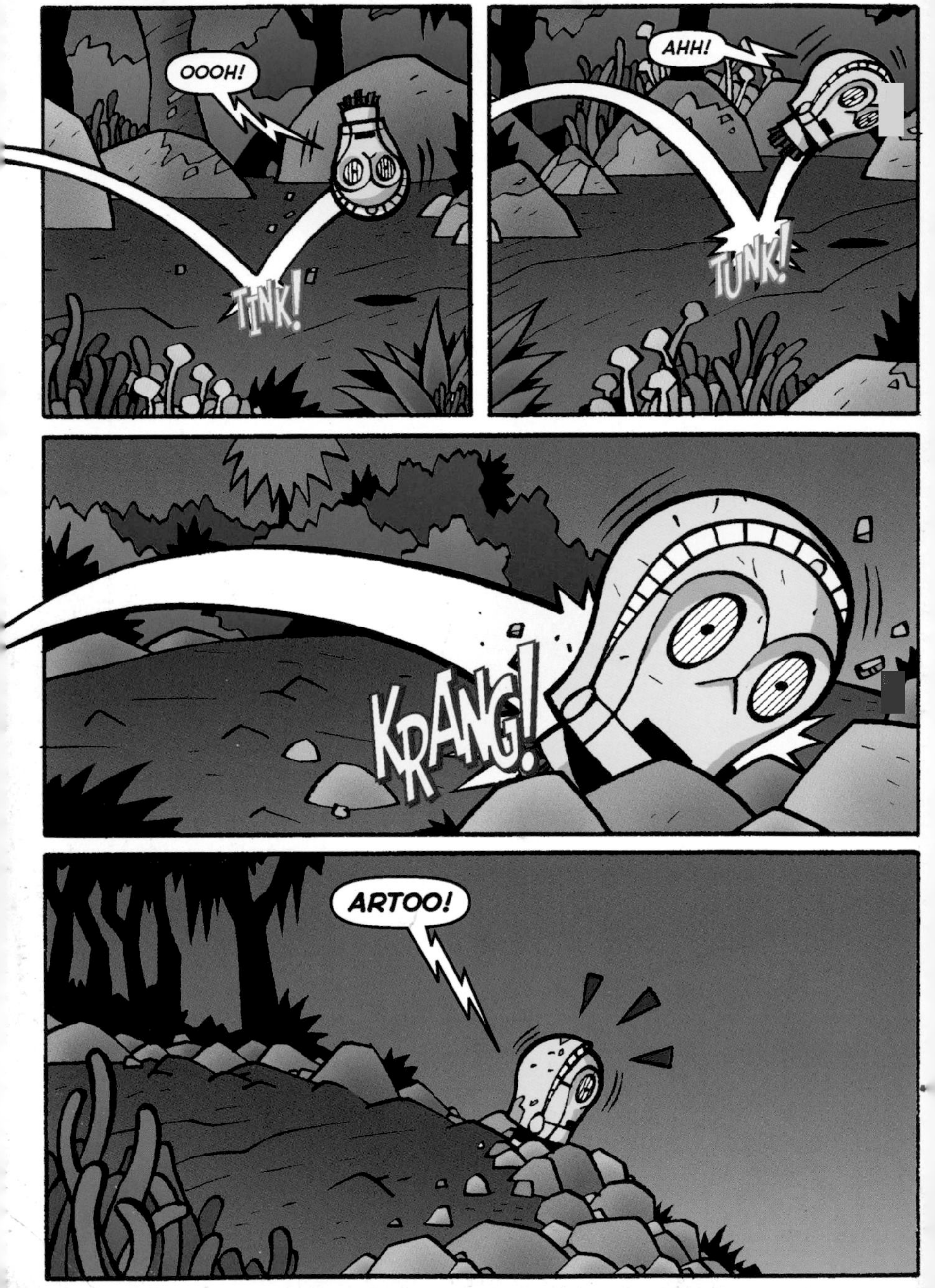
OOOH!
TINK!
AHH!
TUNK!
KRANG!
ARTOO!

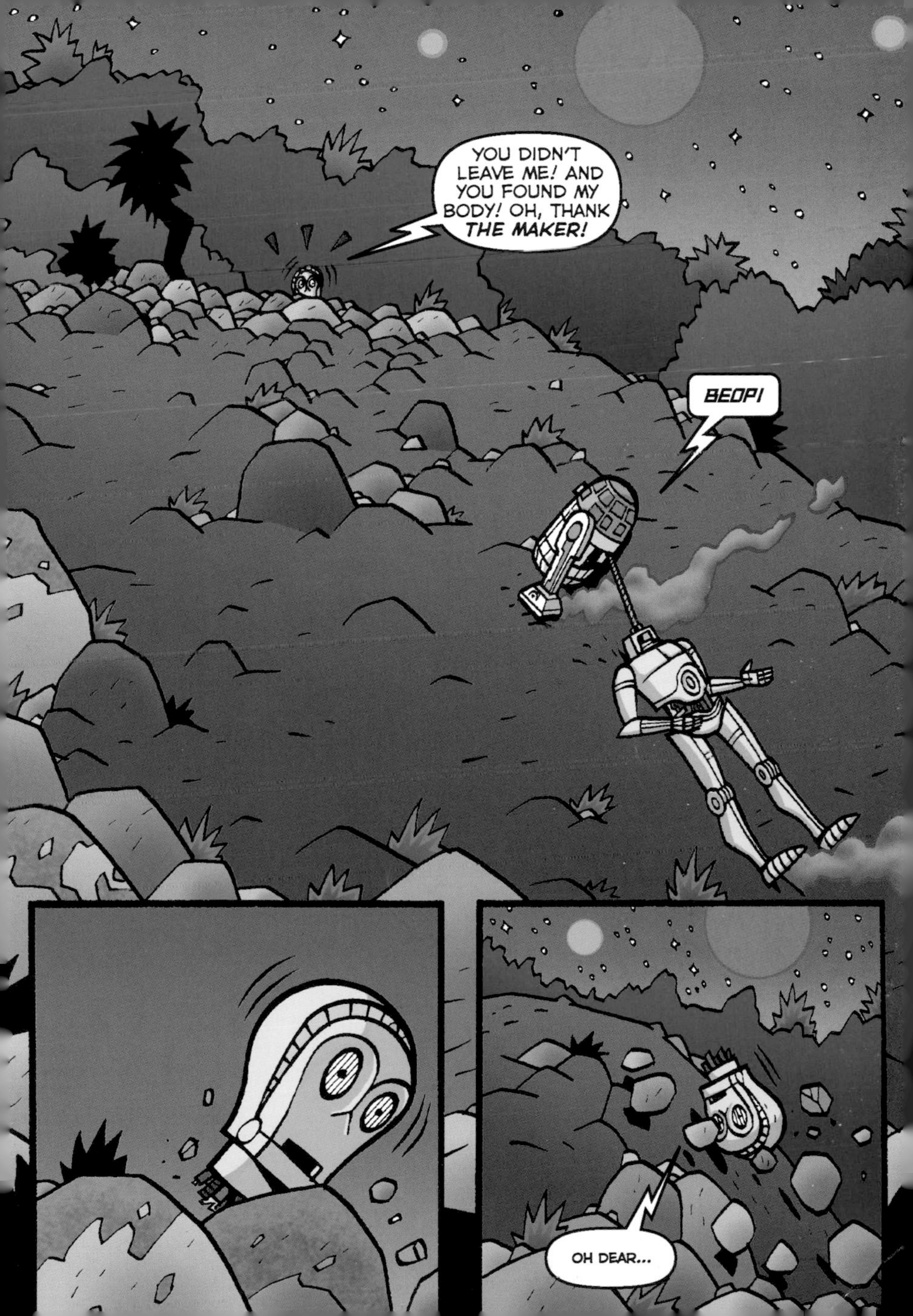
YOU DIDN'T LEAVE ME! AND YOU FOUND MY BODY! OH, THANK *THE MAKER!*
BEOP!
OH DEAR...

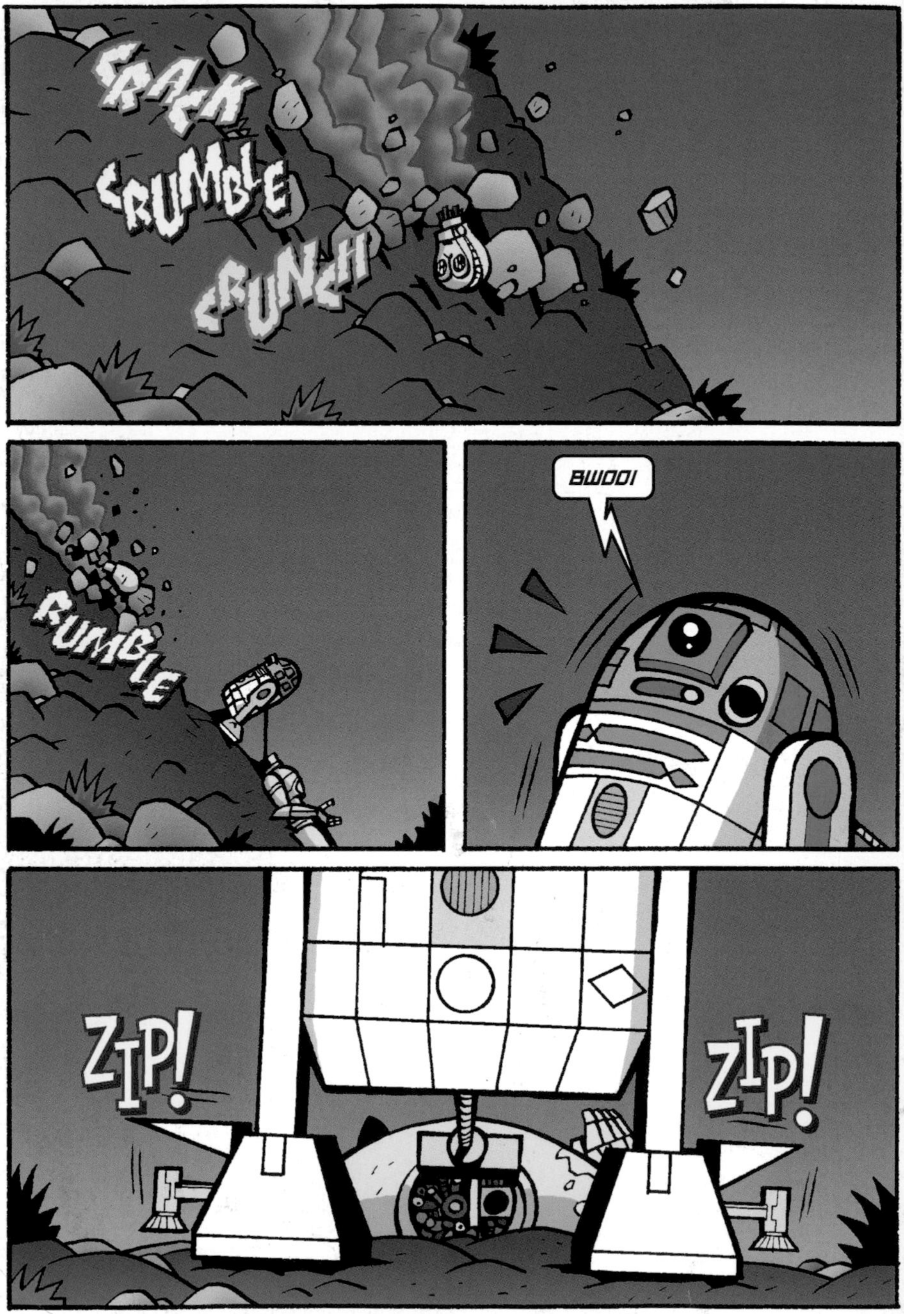
CRACK
CRUMBLE
CRUNCH
RUMBLE
BWOOI
ZIP!
ZIP!

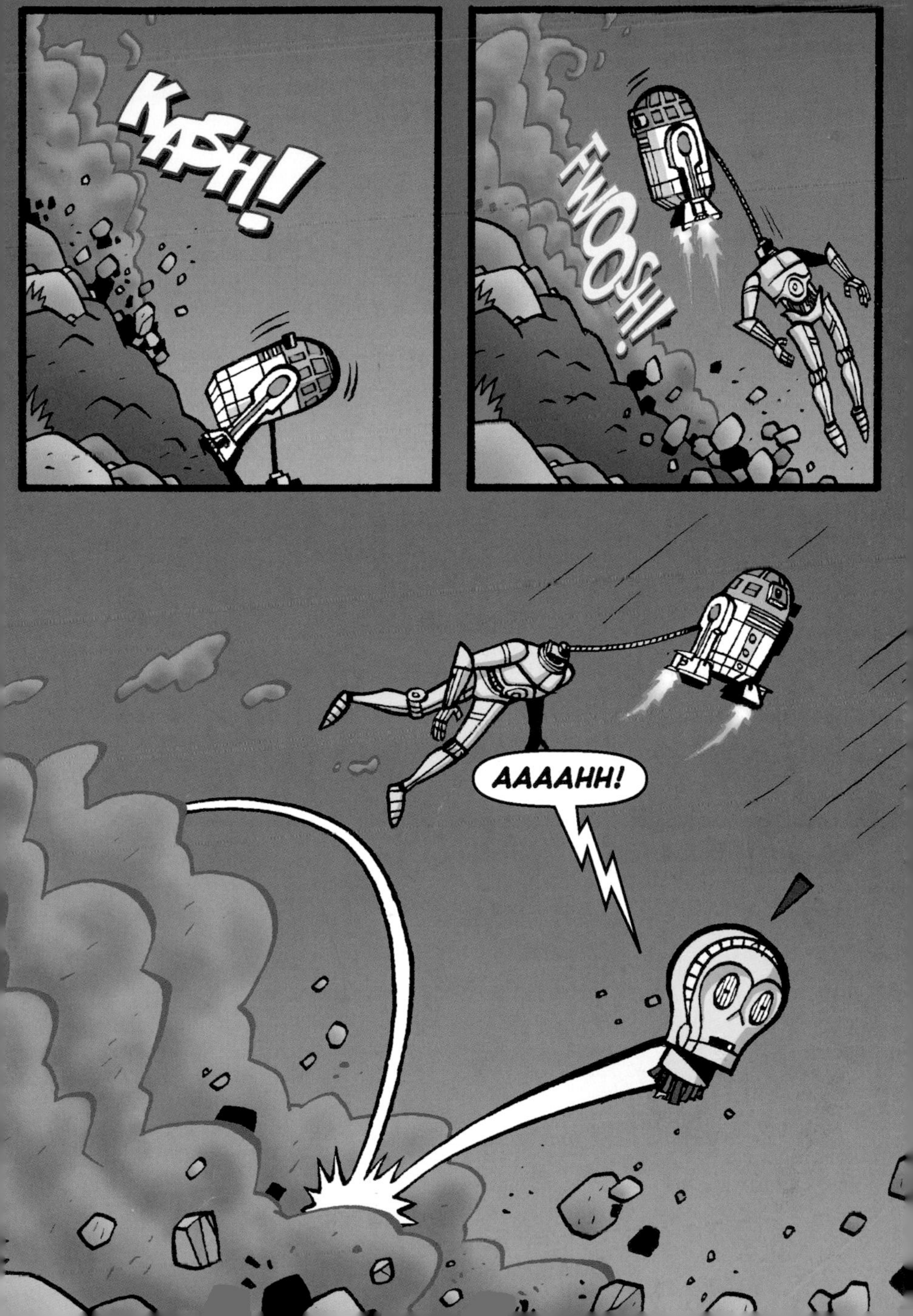
KASH!
FWOOSH!!
AAAAHH!

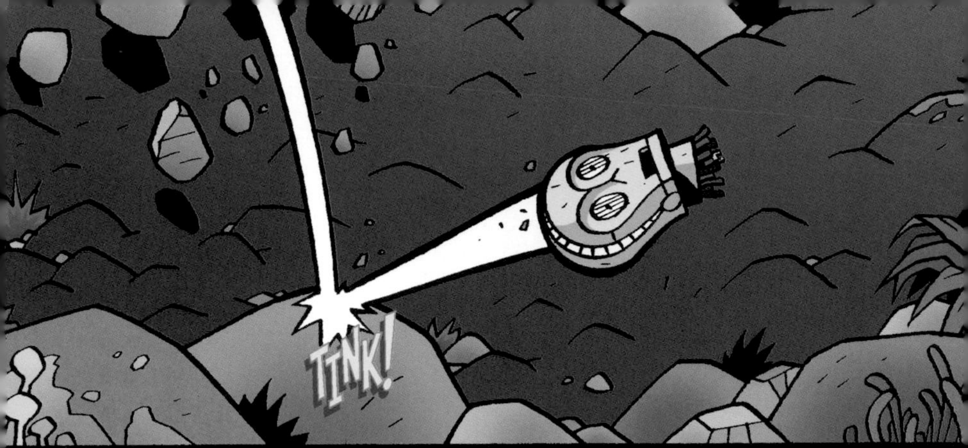
TINK!

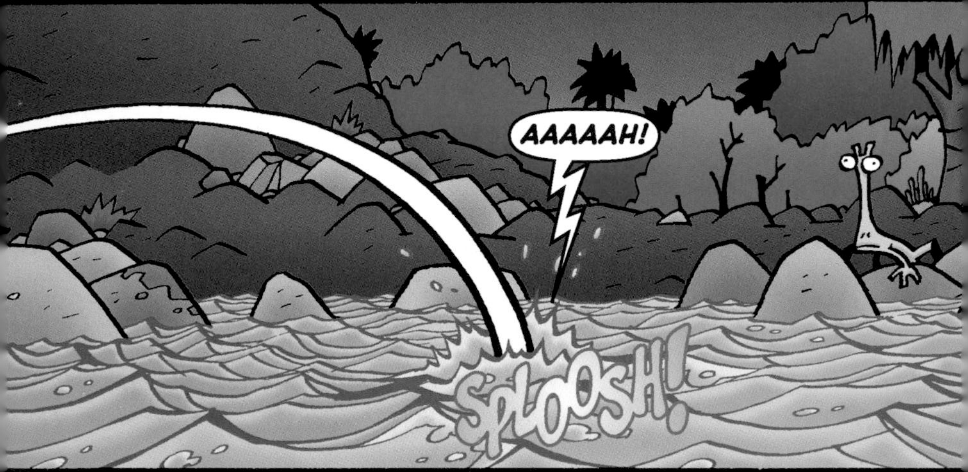
AAAAAH!
SPLOOSH!

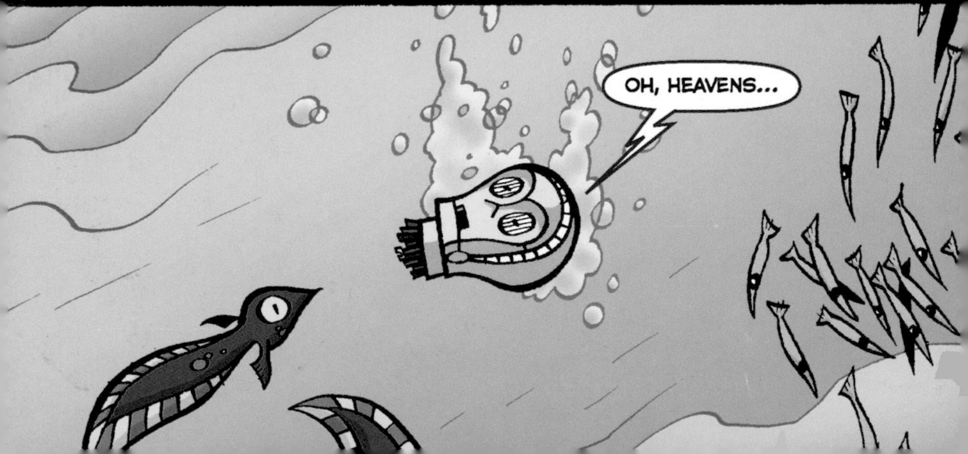
OH, HEAVENS...

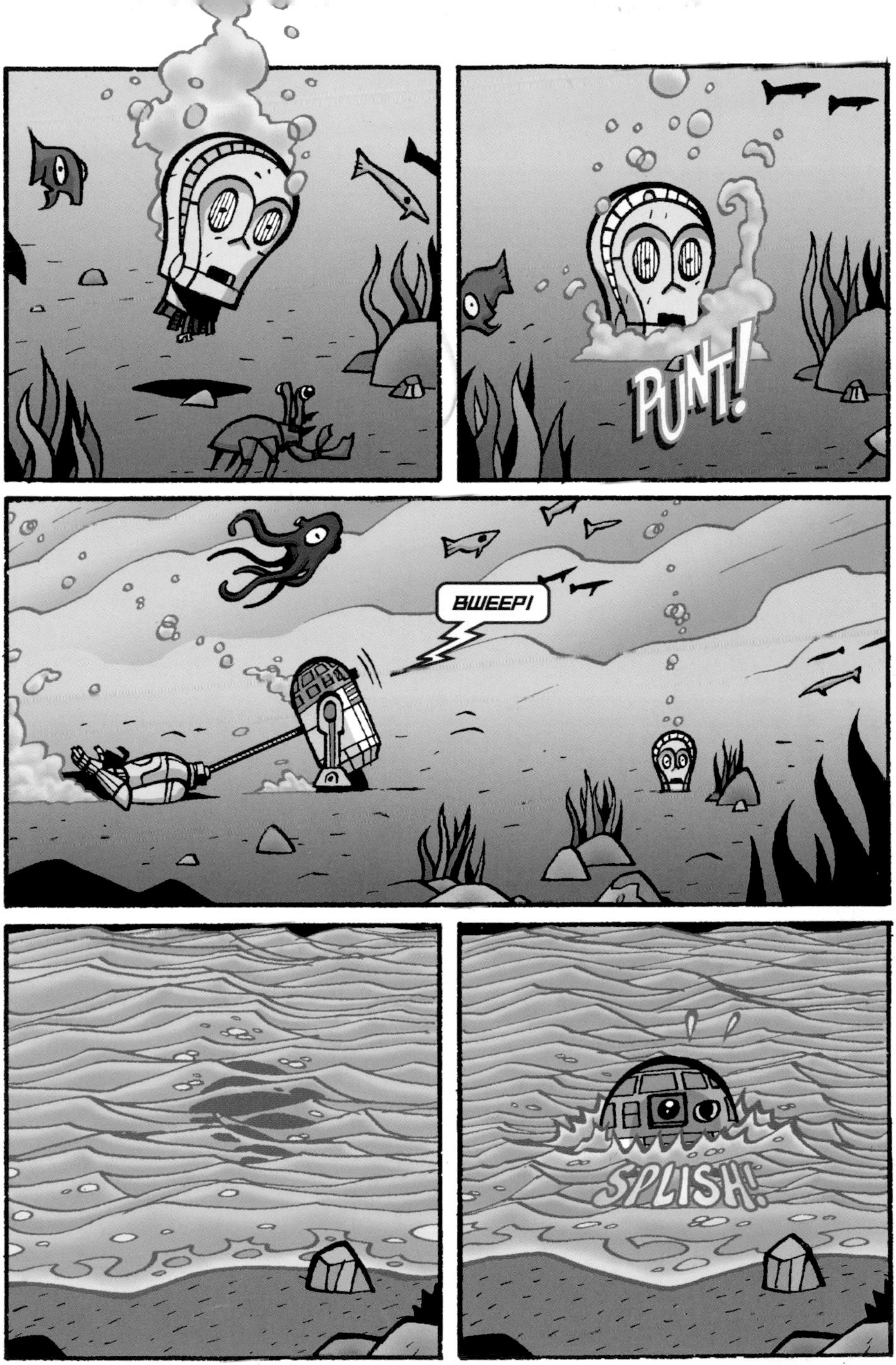
PUNT!
BWEEP!
SPLISH!

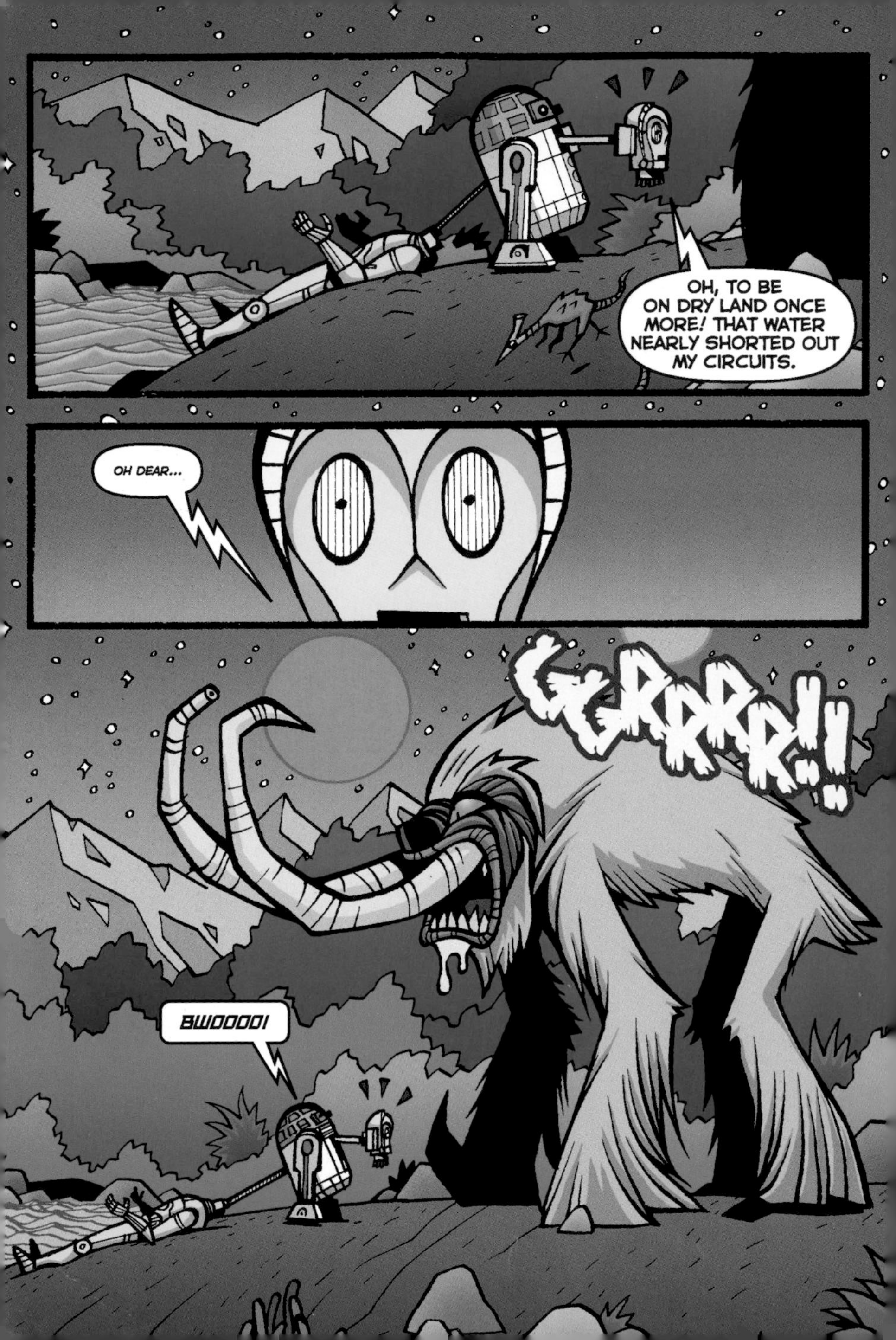
OH, TO BE ON DRY LAND ONCE MORE! THAT WATER NEARLY SHORTED OUT MY CIRCUITS.
OH DEAR...
GERRRR!!
BWOOOO!

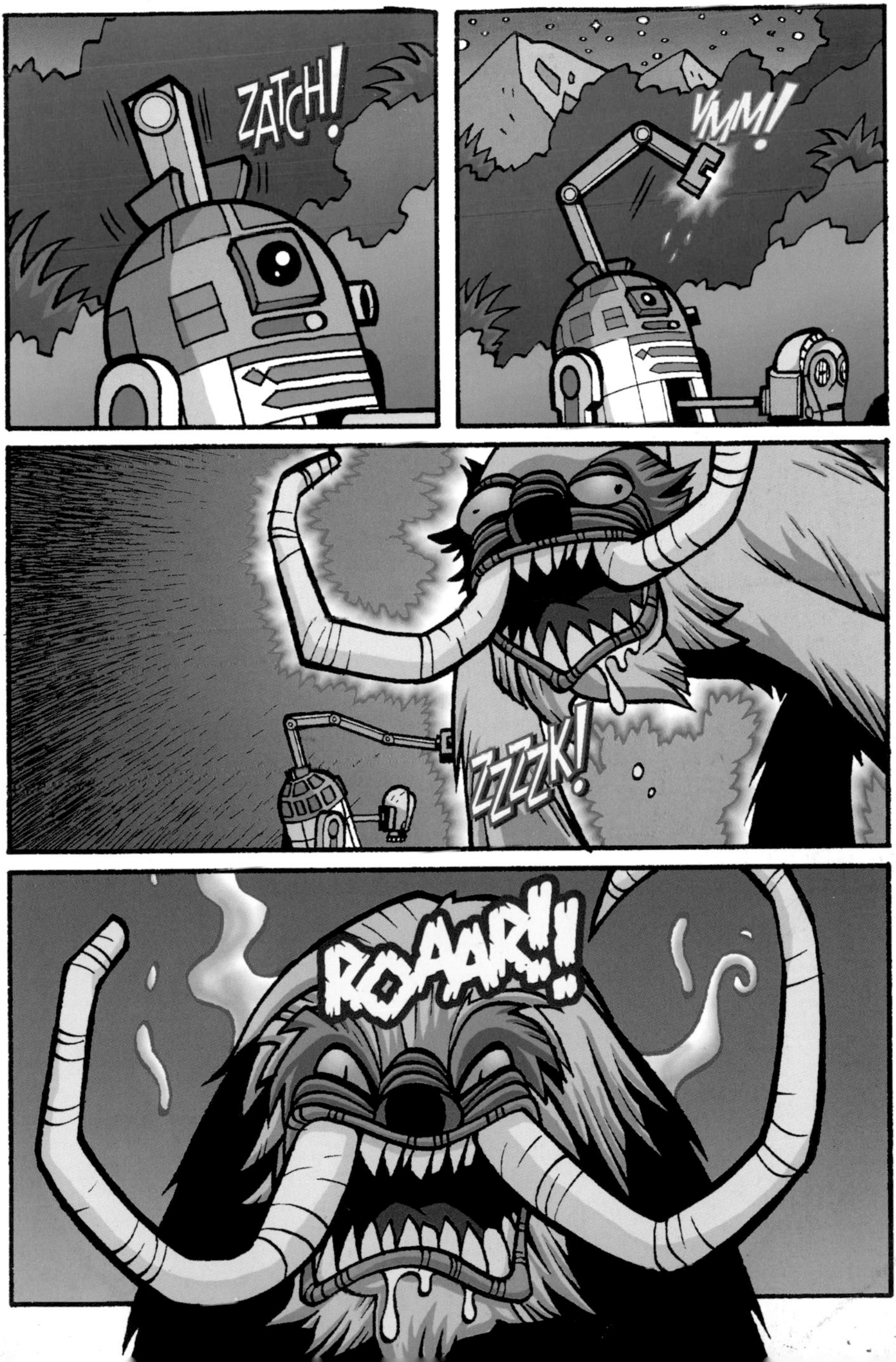
ZATCH!
VMM!
ZZZZK!
ROAAR!!

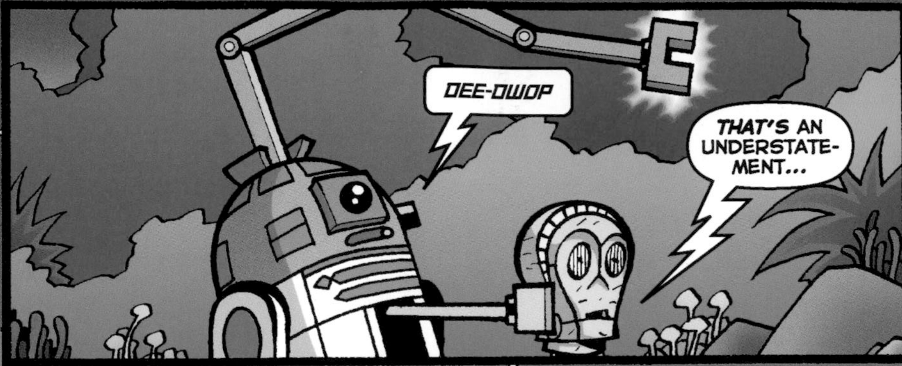
DEE-DWOP
THAT'S AN UNDERSTATE-MENT...

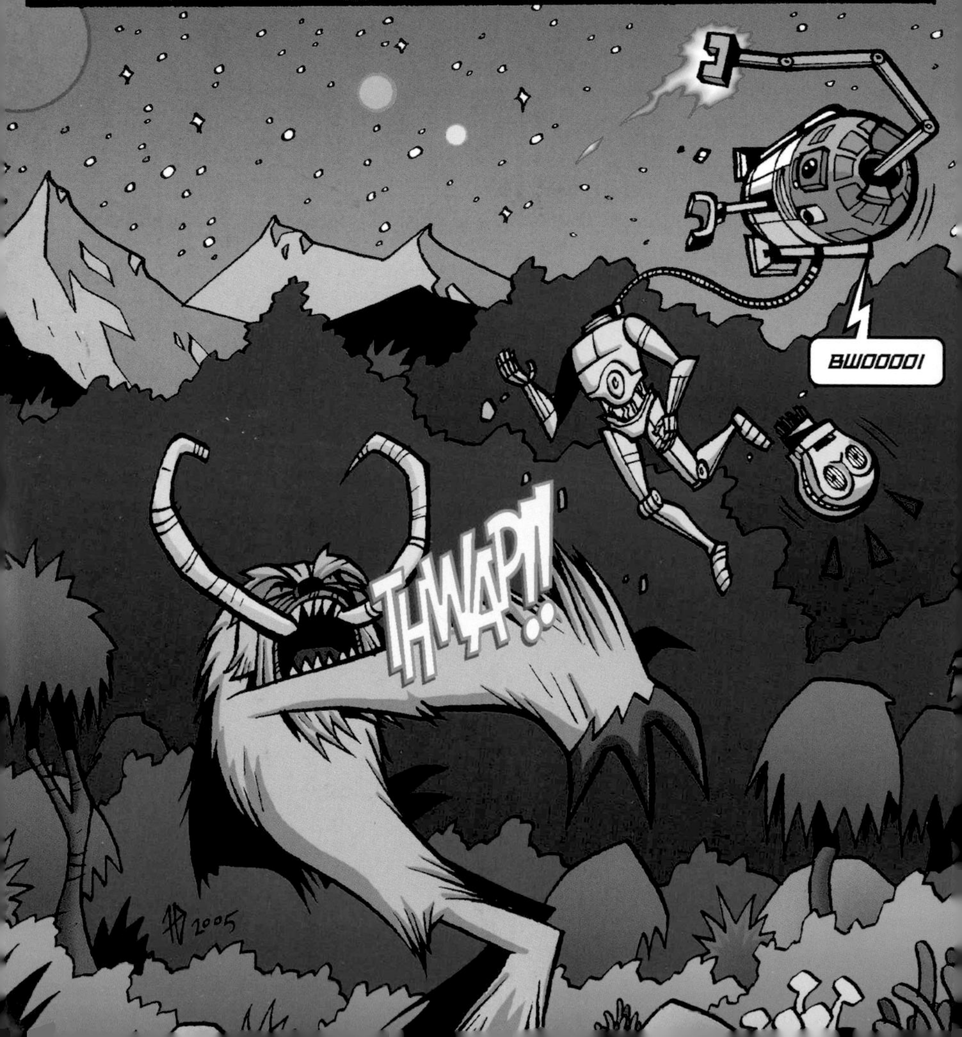
BWOOOO!
THWAP!!

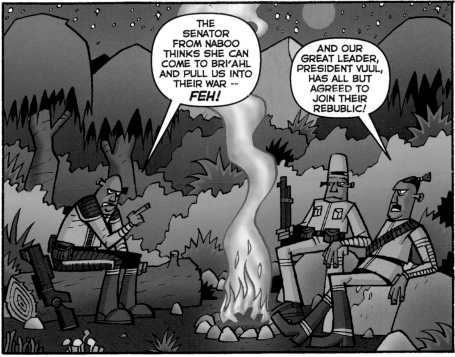

THE SENATOR FROM NABOO THINKS SHE CAN COME TO BRI'AHL AND PULL US INTO THEIR WAR -- *FEH!*

AND OUR GREAT LEADER, PRESIDENT VUUL, HAS ALL BUT AGREED TO JOIN THEIR REBUBLIC!

DESPERATE TIMES CALL FOR DRASTIC MEASURES...

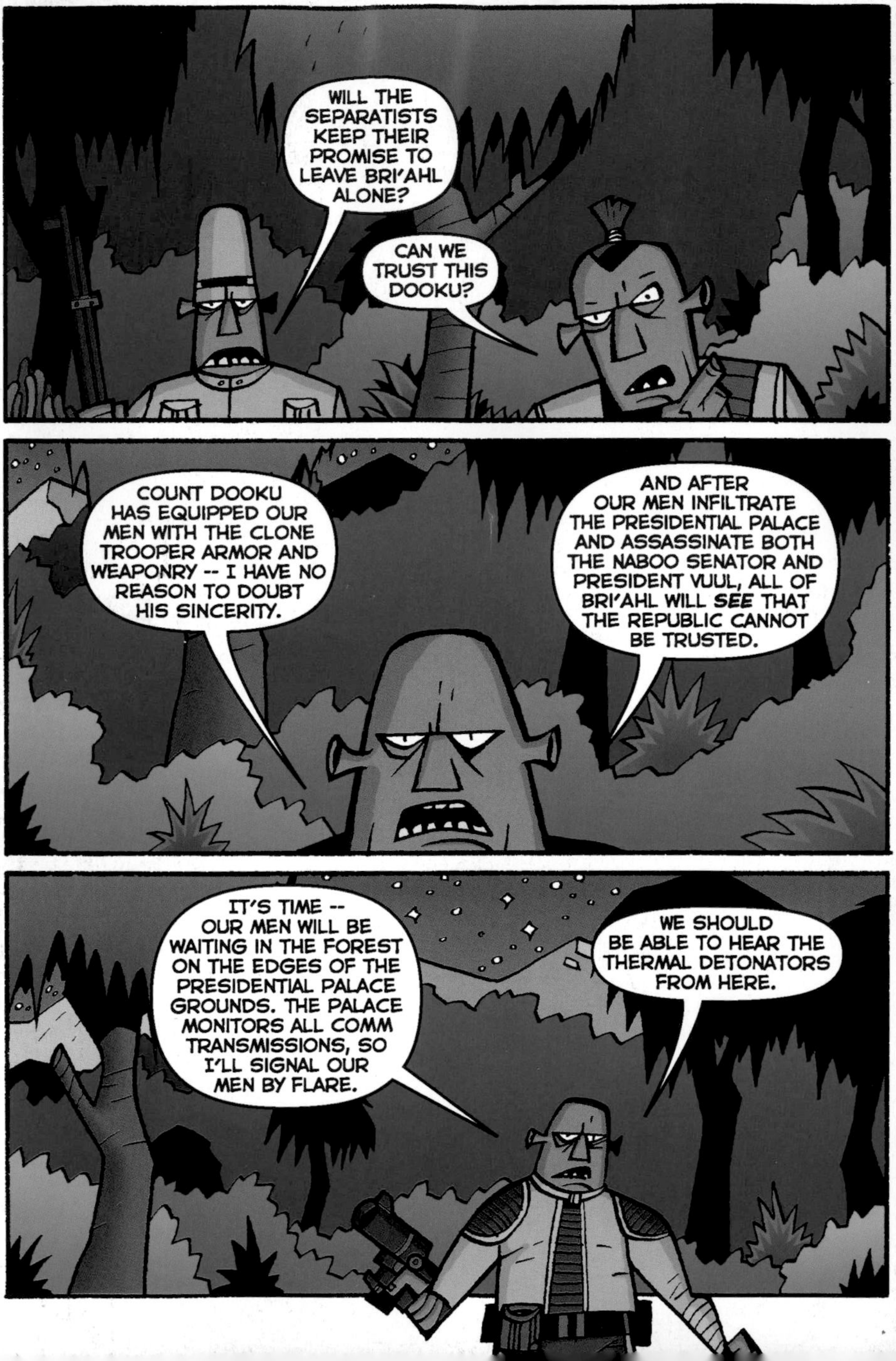
WILL THE SEPARATISTS KEEP THEIR PROMISE TO LEAVE BRI'AHL ALONE?
CAN WE TRUST THIS DOOKU?
COUNT DOOKU HAS EQUIPPED OUR MEN WITH THE CLONE TROOPER ARMOR AND WEAPONRY -- I HAVE NO REASON TO DOUBT HIS SINCERITY.
AND AFTER OUR MEN INFILTRATE THE PRESIDENTIAL PALACE AND ASSASSINATE BOTH THE NABOO SENATOR AND PRESIDENT VUUL, ALL OF BRI'AHL WILL *SEE* THAT THE REPUBLIC CANNOT BE TRUSTED.
IT'S TIME -- OUR MEN WILL BE WAITING IN THE FOREST ON THE EDGES OF THE PRESIDENTIAL PALACE GROUNDS. THE PALACE MONITORS ALL COMM TRANSMISSIONS, SO I'LL SIGNAL OUR MEN BY FLARE.
WE SHOULD BE ABLE TO HEAR THE THERMAL DETONATORS FROM HERE.

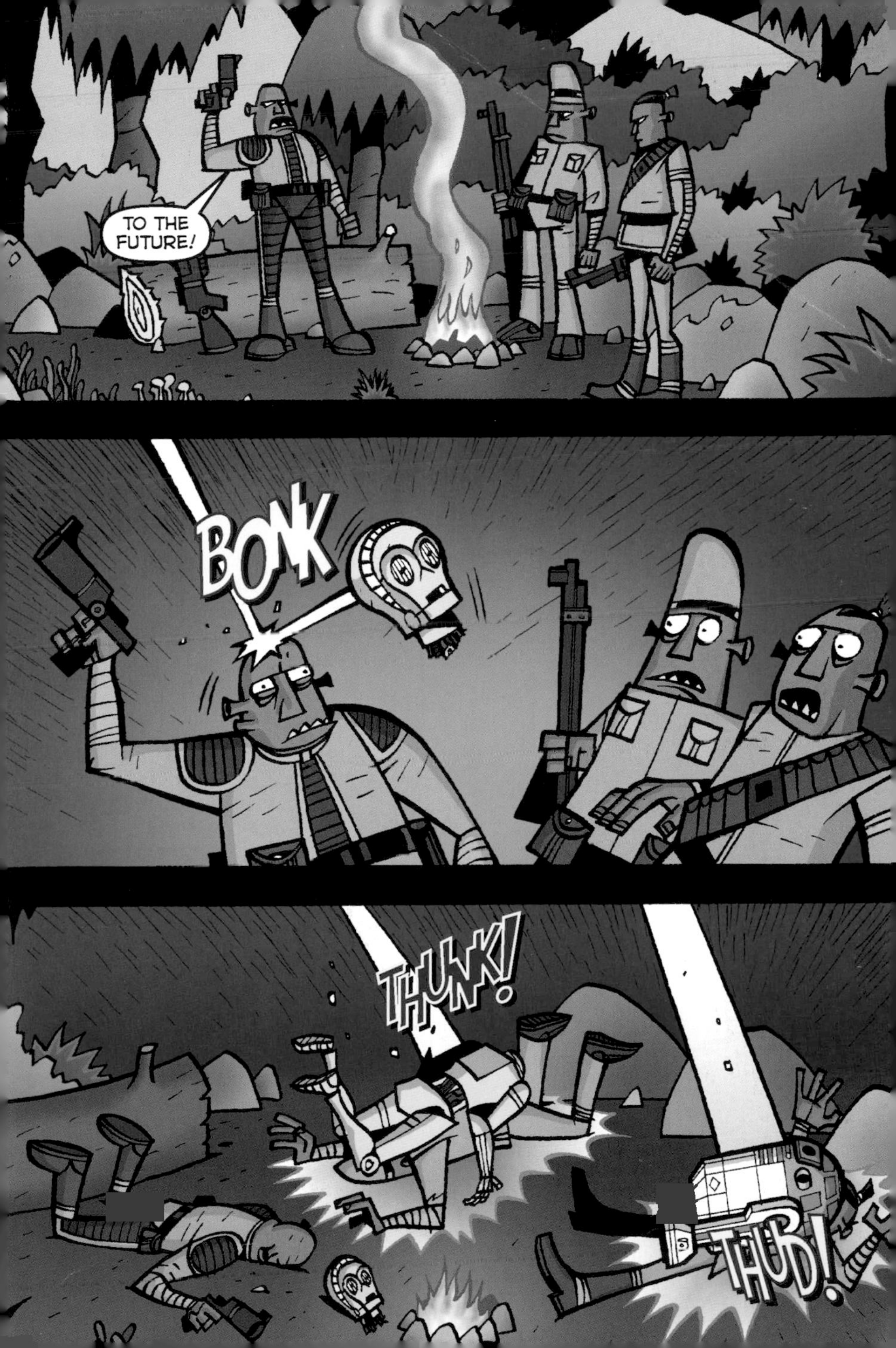
TO THE FUTURE!
BONK
THUNK!
THUD!

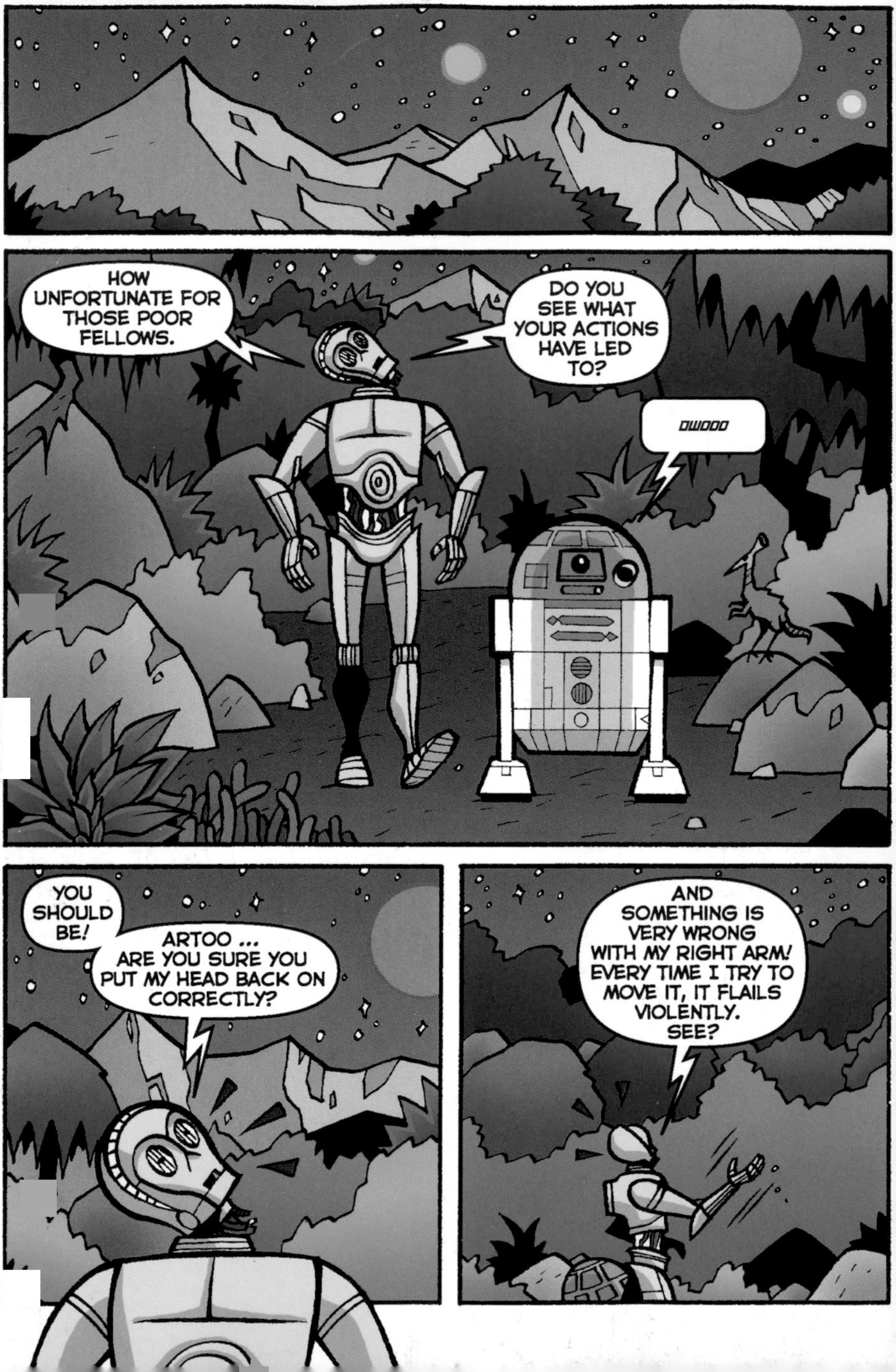
HOW UNFORTUNATE FOR THOSE POOR FELLOWS.
DO YOU SEE WHAT YOUR ACTIONS HAVE LED TO?
DWOOO
YOU SHOULD BE!
ARTOO ... ARE YOU SURE YOU PUT MY HEAD BACK ON CORRECTLY?
AND SOMETHING IS VERY WRONG WITH MY RIGHT ARM! EVERY TIME I TRY TO MOVE IT, IT FLAILS VIOLENTLY. SEE?

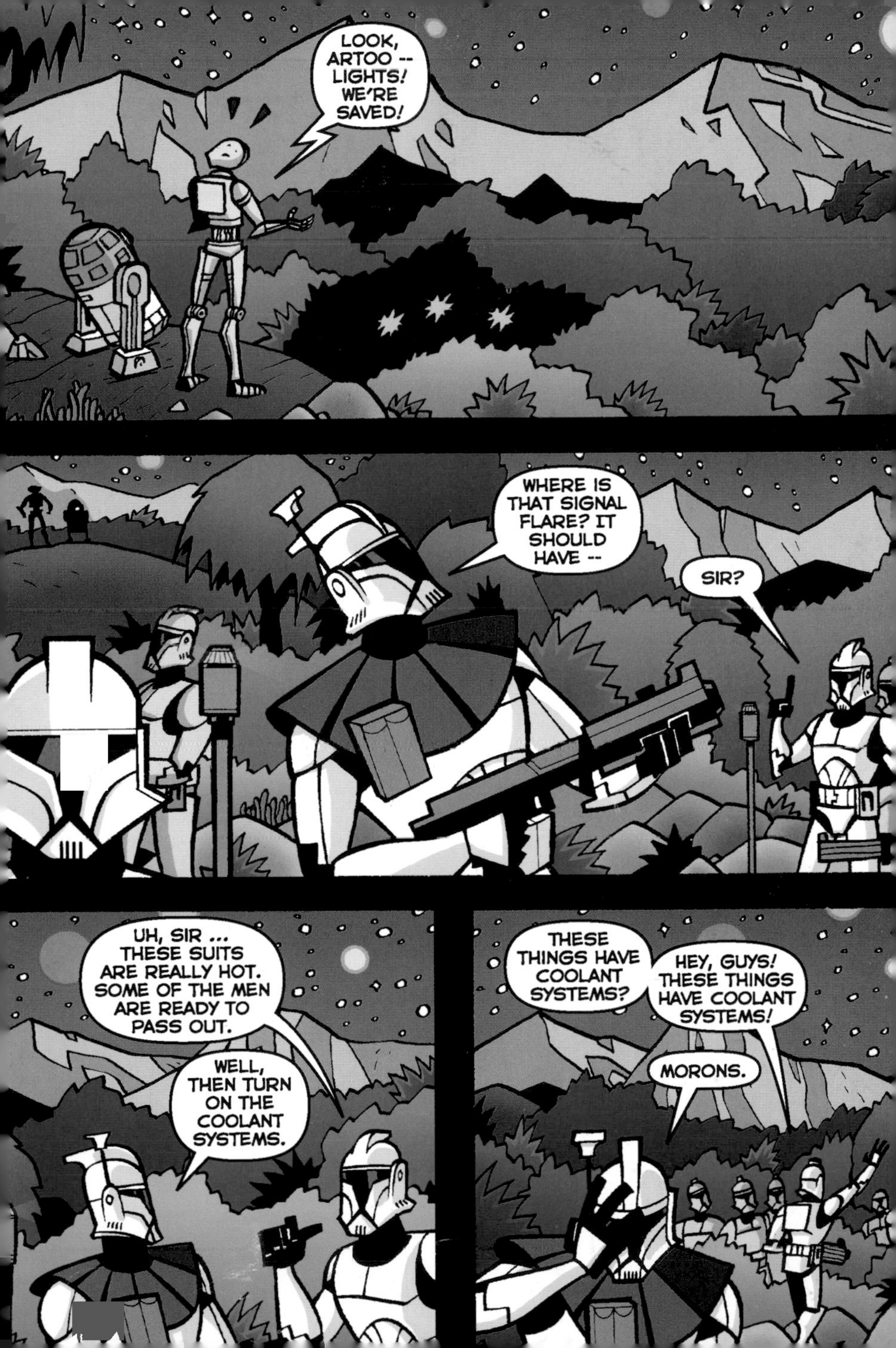
LOOK, ARTOO -- LIGHTS! WE'RE SAVED!
WHERE IS THAT SIGNAL FLARE? IT SHOULD HAVE --
SIR?
UH, SIR ... THESE SUITS ARE REALLY HOT. SOME OF THE MEN ARE READY TO PASS OUT.
WELL, THEN TURN ON THE COOLANT SYSTEMS.
THESE THINGS HAVE COOLANT SYSTEMS?
HEY, GUYS! THESE THINGS HAVE COOLANT SYSTEMS!
MORONS.

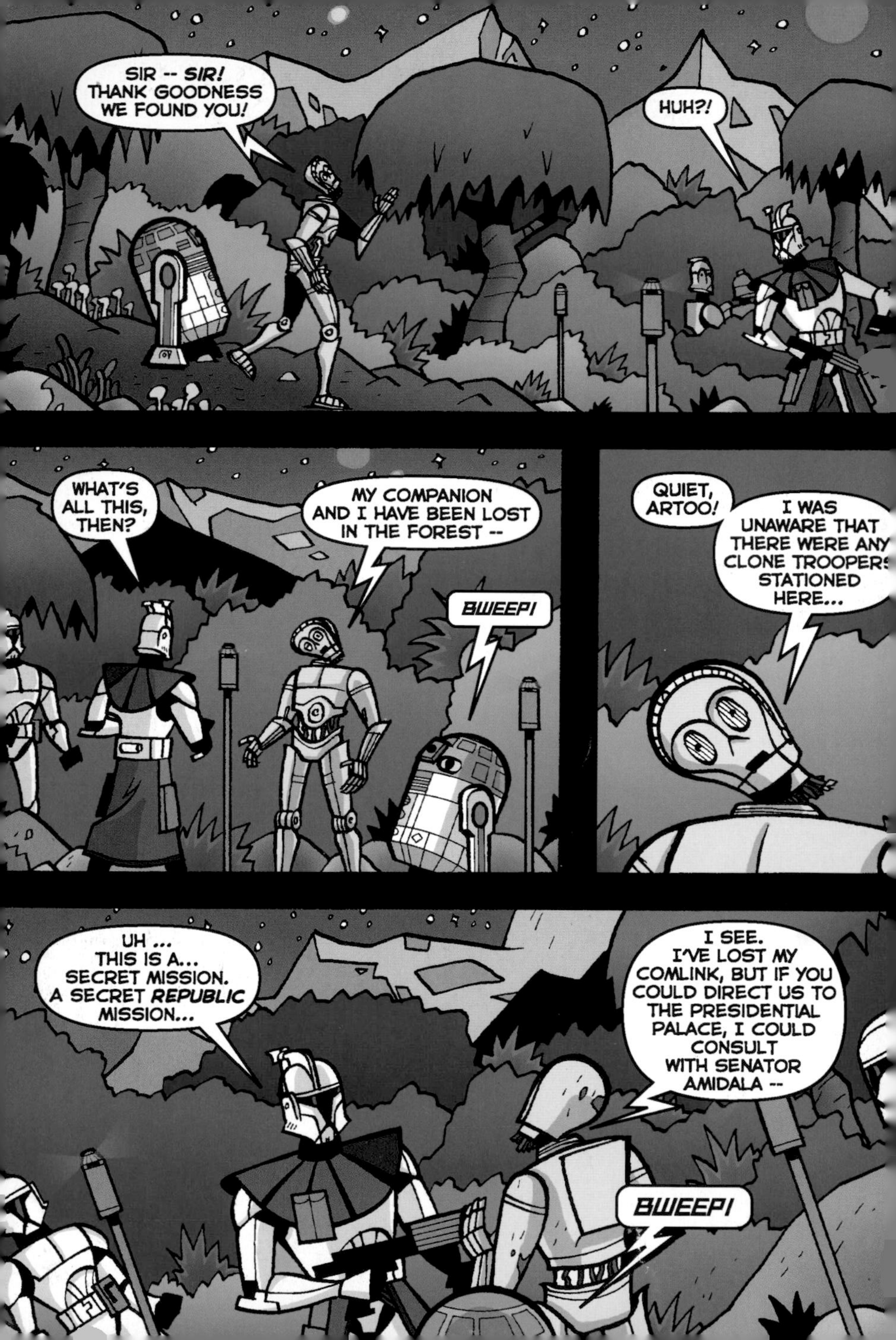
SIR -- SIR! THANK GOODNESS WE FOUND YOU!
HUH?!
WHAT'S ALL THIS, THEN?
MY COMPANION AND I HAVE BEEN LOST IN THE FOREST --
BWEEP!
QUIET, ARTOO!
I WAS UNAWARE THAT THERE WERE ANY CLONE TROOPERS STATIONED HERE...
UH ... THIS IS A... SECRET MISSION. A SECRET REPUBLIC MISSION...
I SEE. I'VE LOST MY COMLINK, BUT IF YOU COULD DIRECT US TO THE PRESIDENTIAL PALACE, I COULD CONSULT WITH SENATOR AMIDALA --
BWEEP!

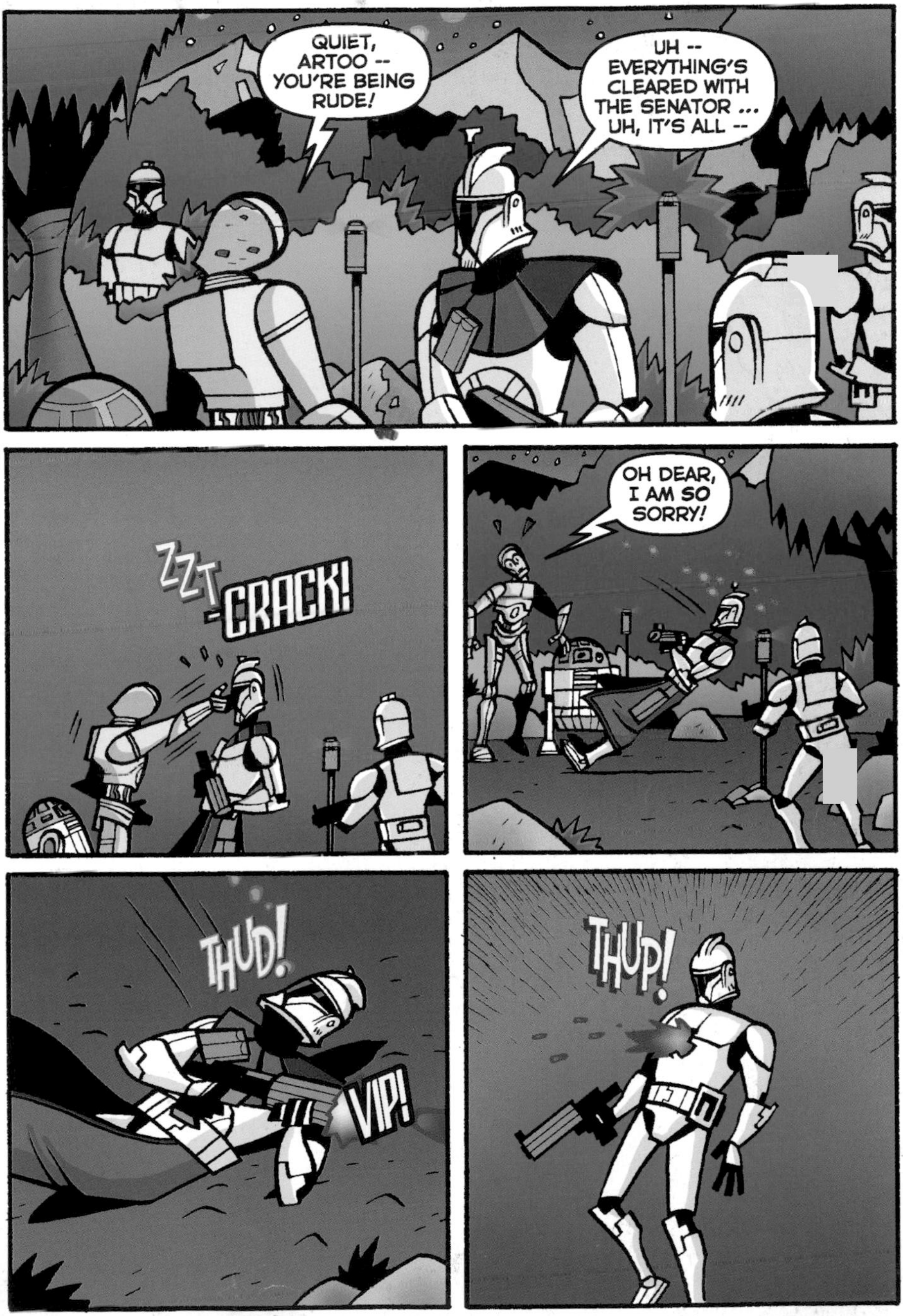
QUIET, ARTOO -- YOU'RE BEING RUDE!
UH -- EVERYTHING'S CLEARED WITH THE SENATOR ... UH, IT'S ALL --
ZZT-CRACK!
OH DEAR, I AM SO SORRY!
THUD!
VIP!
THUP!

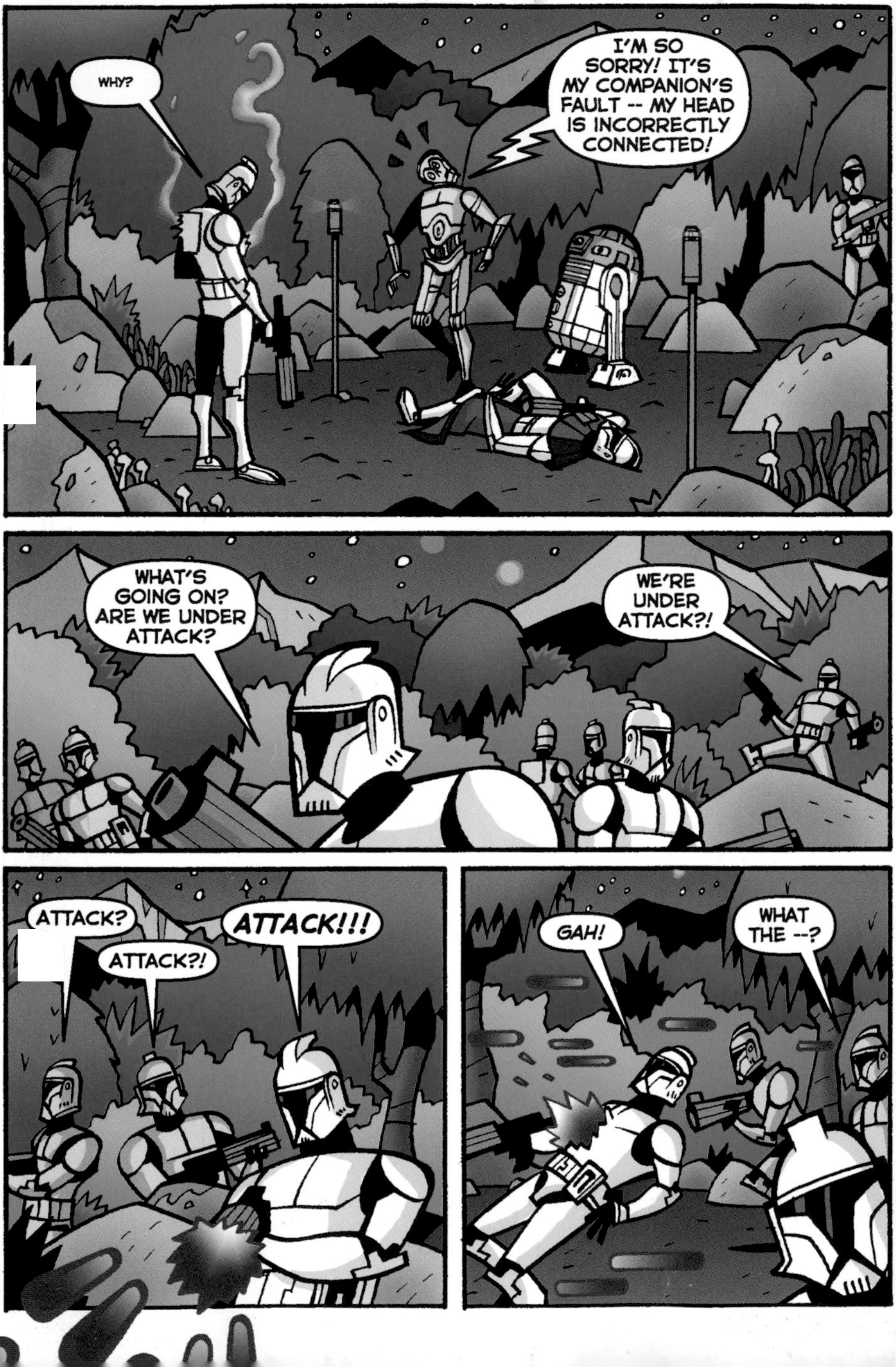
WHY?
I'M SO SORRY! IT'S MY COMPANION'S FAULT -- MY HEAD IS INCORRECTLY CONNECTED!
WHAT'S GOING ON? ARE WE UNDER ATTACK?
WE'RE UNDER ATTACK?!
ATTACK?
ATTACK?!
ATTACK!!!
GAH!
WHAT THE --?

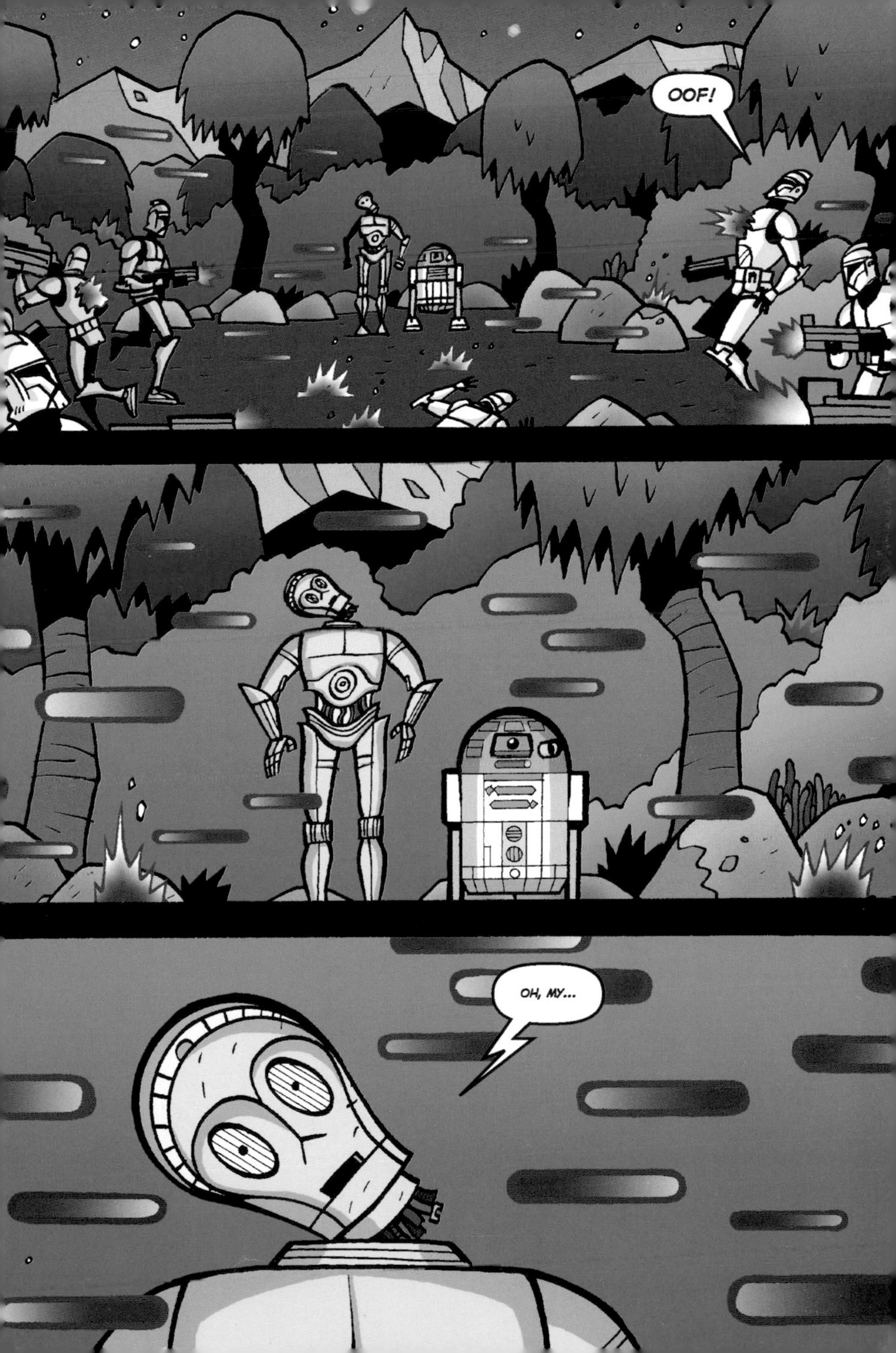
OOF!
OH, MY...

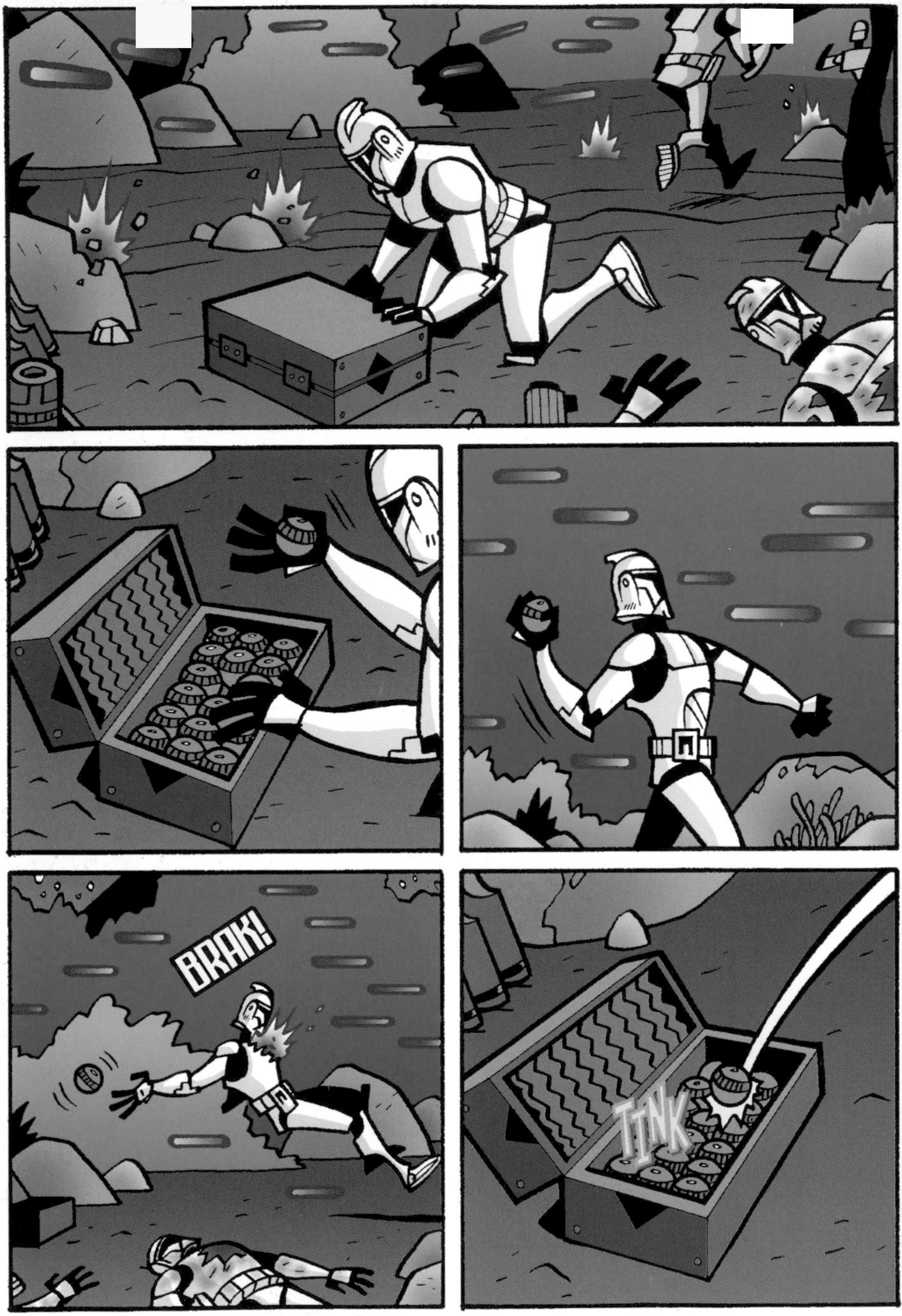
BRAK!
TINK

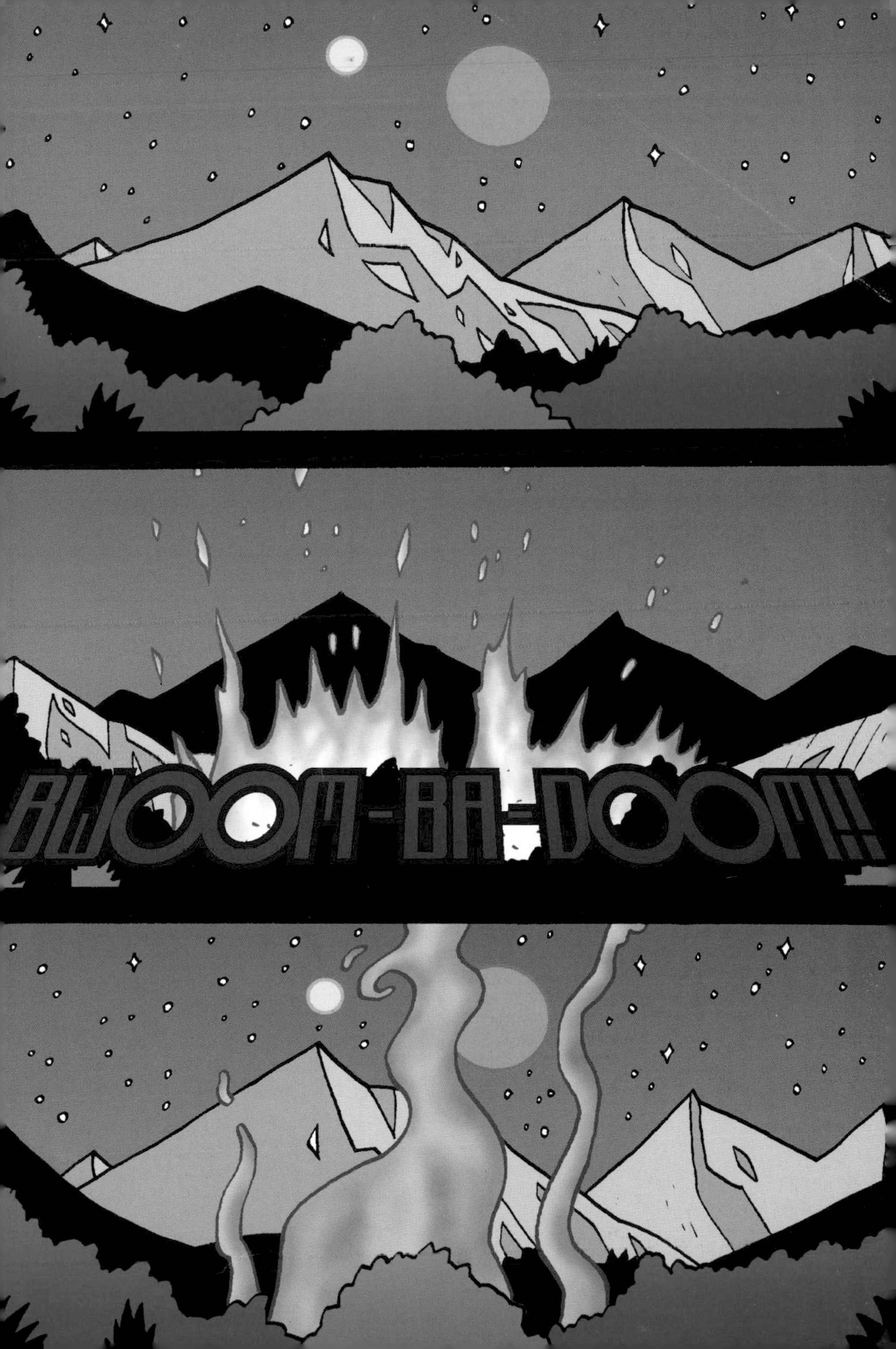
BWOOM-BA-DOOM!!

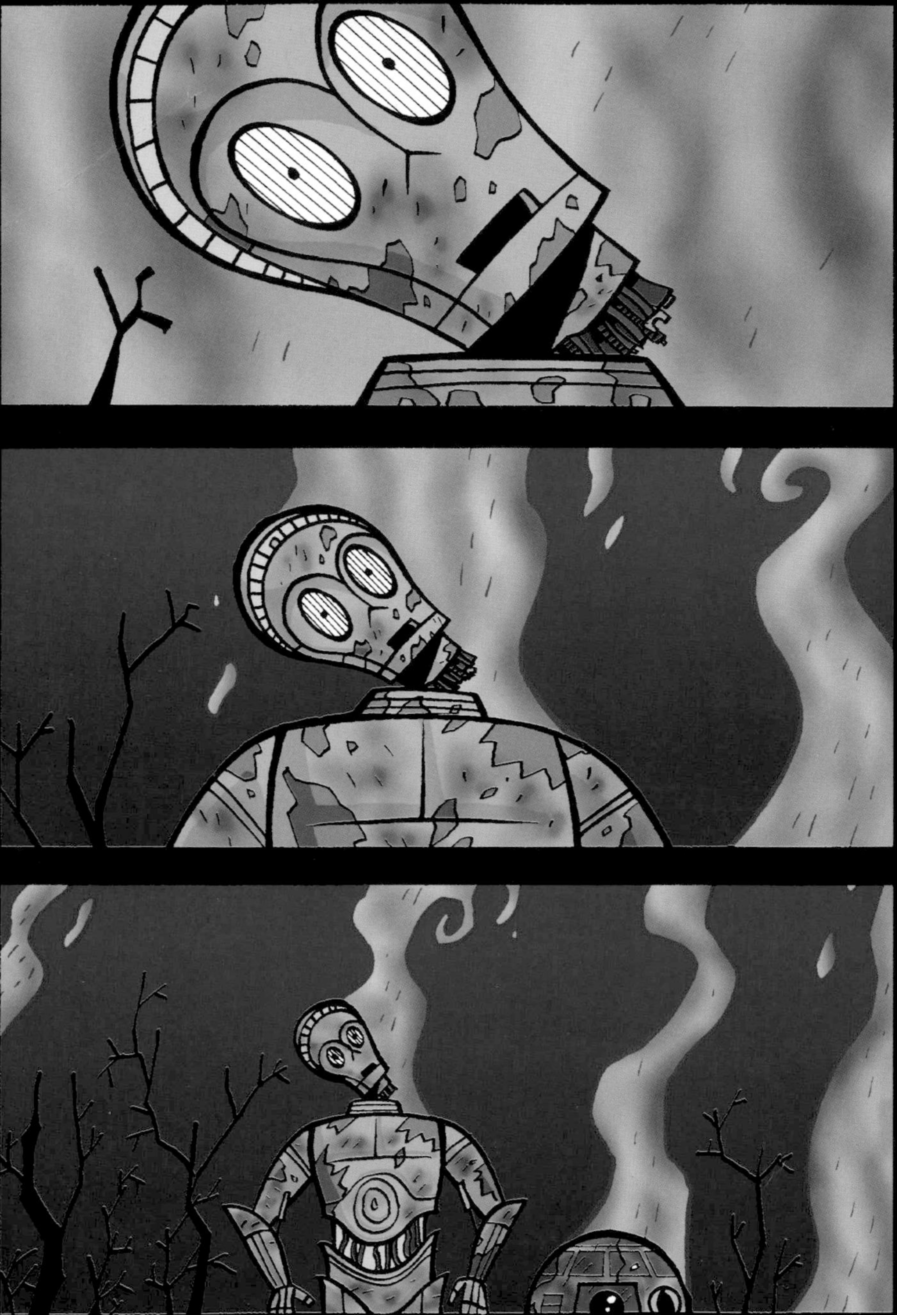

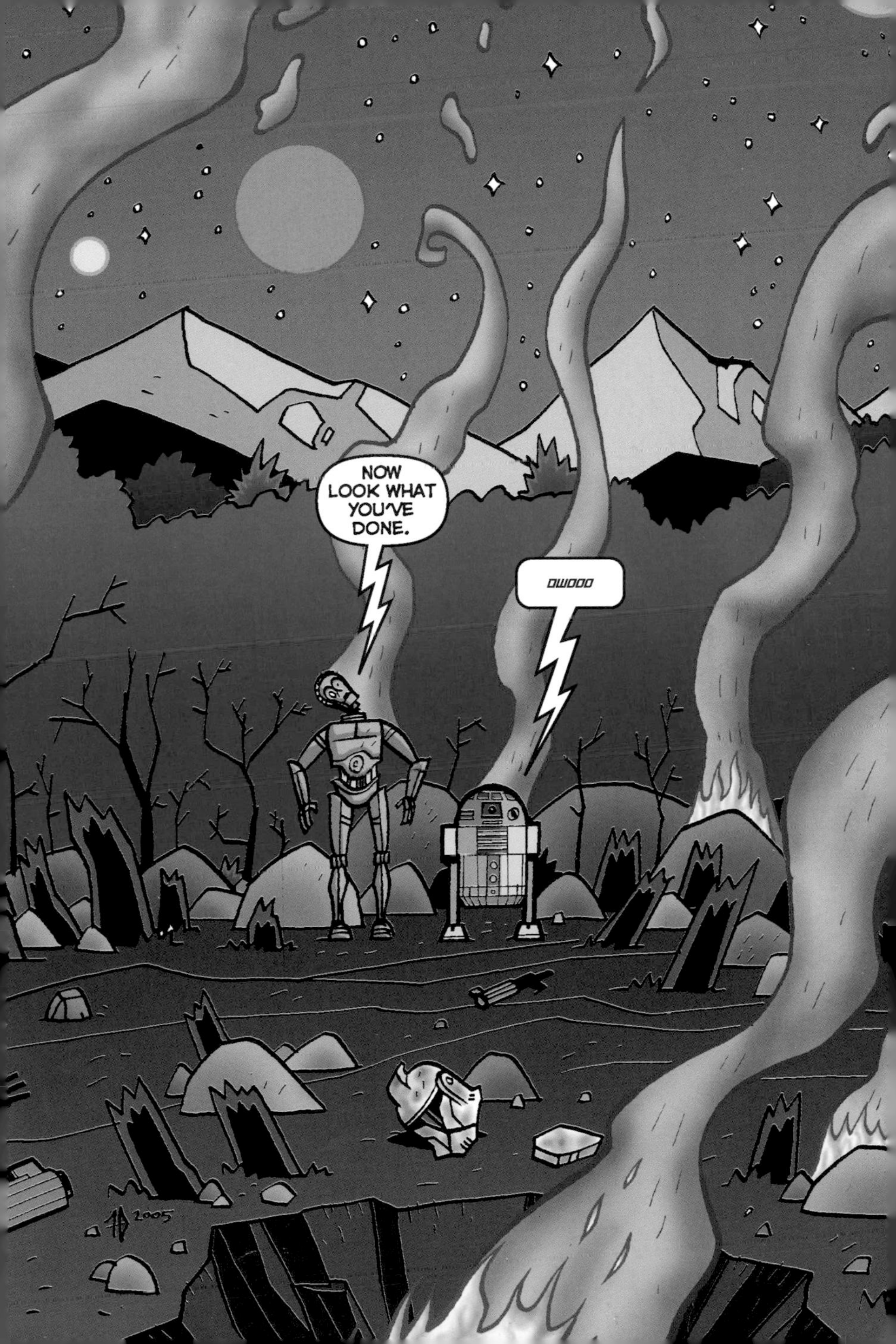
NOW LOOK WHAT YOU'VE DONE.
OWOOO

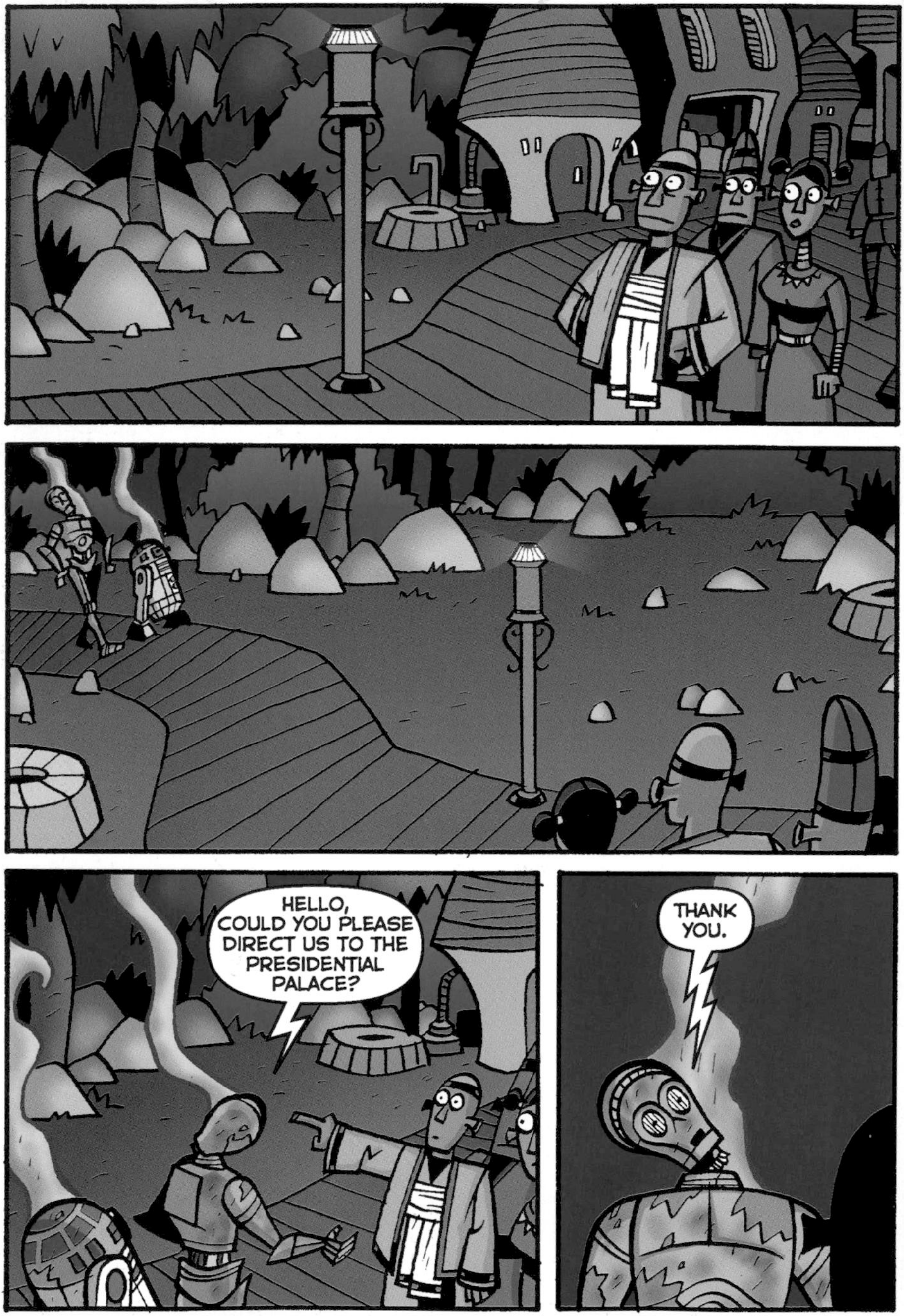
HELLO, COULD YOU PLEASE DIRECT US TO THE PRESIDENTIAL PALACE?
THANK YOU.

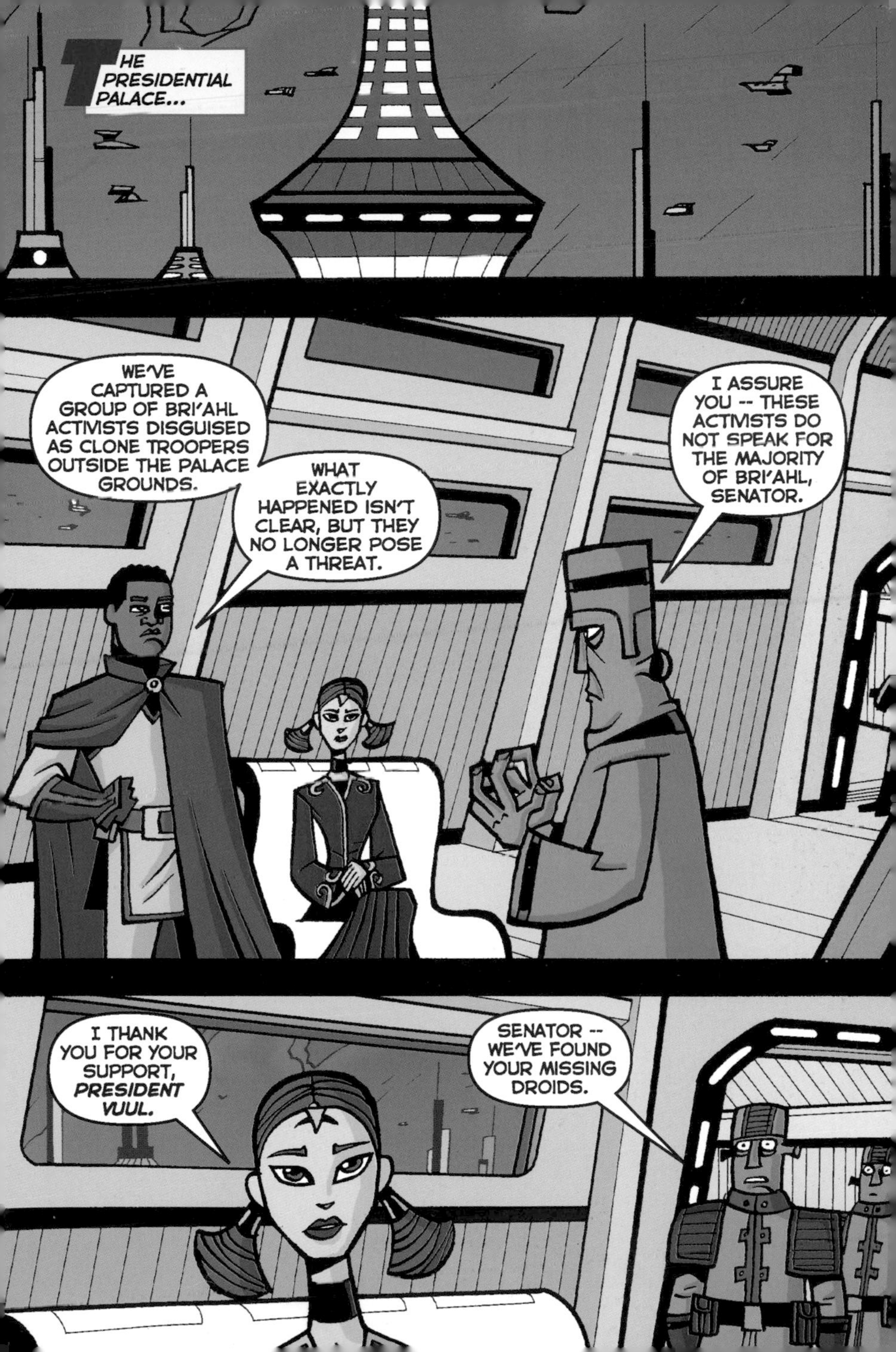
THE PRESIDENTIAL PALACE...
WE'VE CAPTURED A GROUP OF BRI'AHL ACTIVISTS DISGUISED AS CLONE TROOPERS OUTSIDE THE PALACE GROUNDS.
WHAT EXACTLY HAPPENED ISN'T CLEAR, BUT THEY NO LONGER POSE A THREAT.
I ASSURE YOU -- THESE ACTIVISTS DO NOT SPEAK FOR THE MAJORITY OF BRI'AHL, SENATOR.
I THANK YOU FOR YOUR SUPPORT, *PRESIDENT VUUL.*
SENATOR -- WE'VE FOUND YOUR MISSING DROIDS.

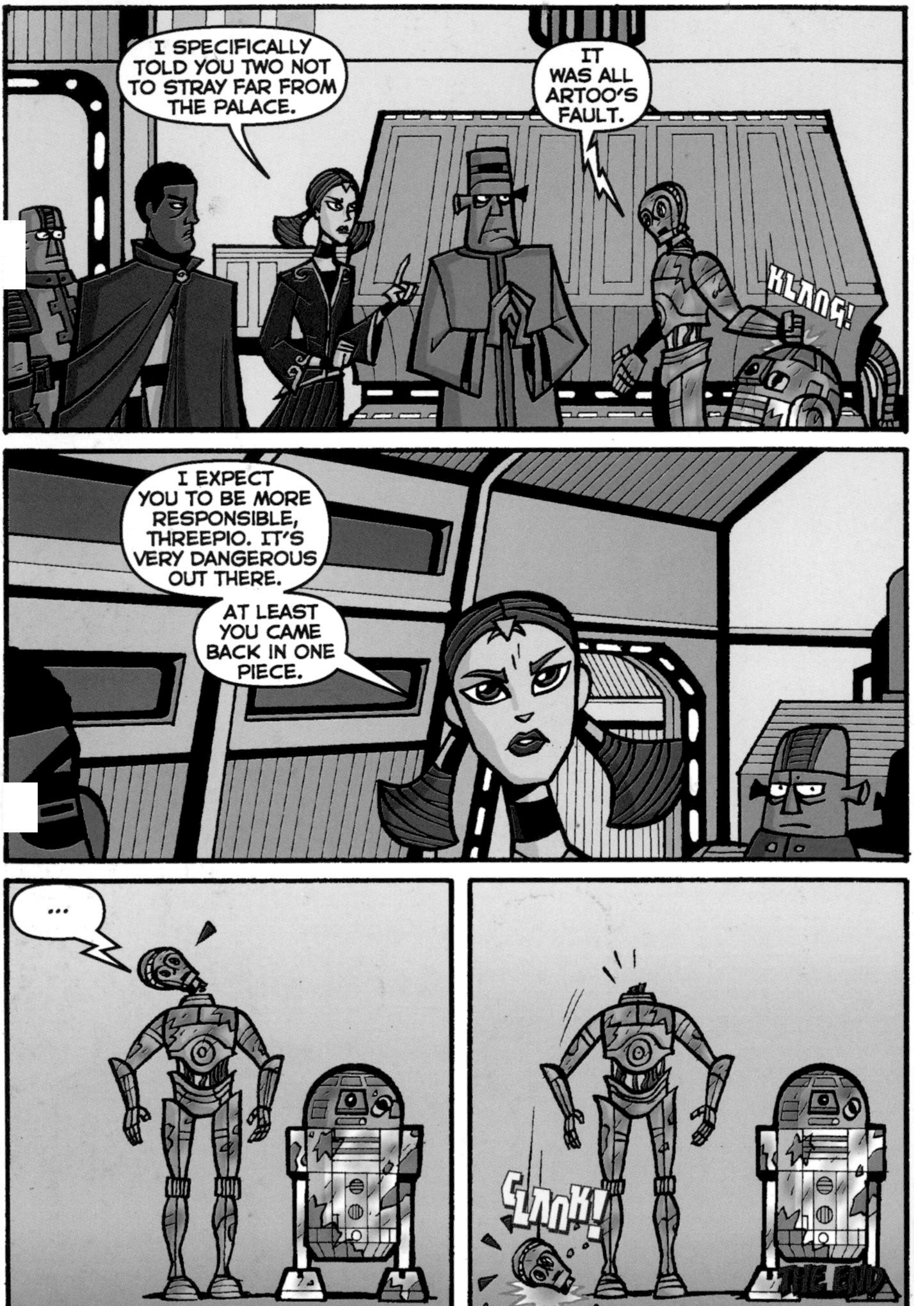
I SPECIFICALLY TOLD YOU TWO NOT TO STRAY FAR FROM THE PALACE.
IT WAS ALL ARTOO'S FAULT.
KLANG!
I EXPECT YOU TO BE MORE RESPONSIBLE, THREEPIO. IT'S VERY DANGEROUS OUT THERE.
AT LEAST YOU CAME BACK IN ONE PIECE.
...
CLANK!
THE END

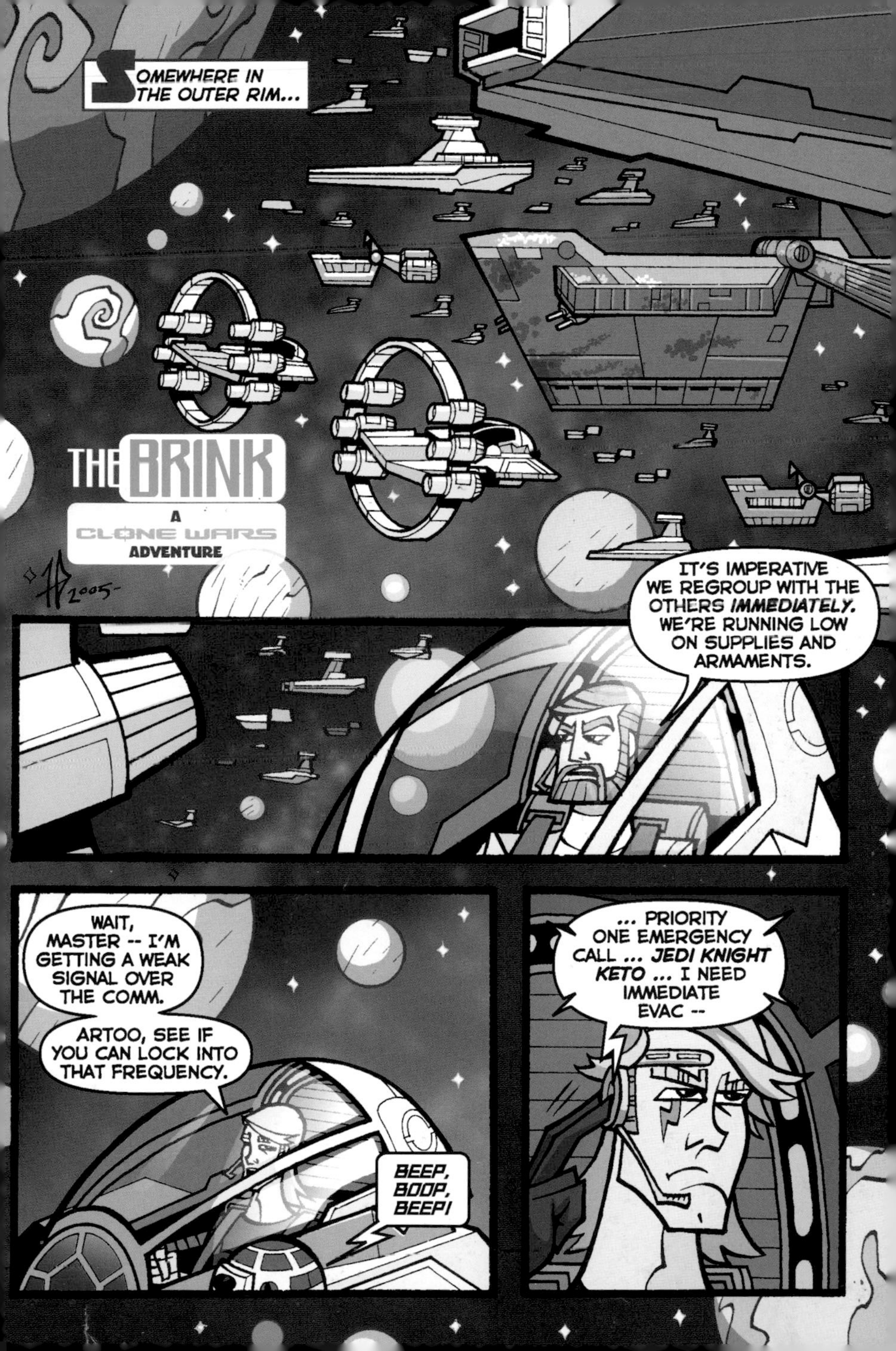
SOMEWHERE IN THE OUTER RIM...
THE BRINK
A CLONE WARS ADVENTURE
IT'S IMPERATIVE WE REGROUP WITH THE OTHERS *IMMEDIATELY.* WE'RE RUNNING LOW ON SUPPLIES AND ARMAMENTS.
WAIT, MASTER -- I'M GETTING A WEAK SIGNAL OVER THE COMM.
ARTOO, SEE IF YOU CAN LOCK INTO THAT FREQUENCY.
BEEP, BOOP, BEEP!
... PRIORITY ONE EMERGENCY CALL ... *JEDI KNIGHT KETO* ... I NEED IMMEDIATE EVAC --

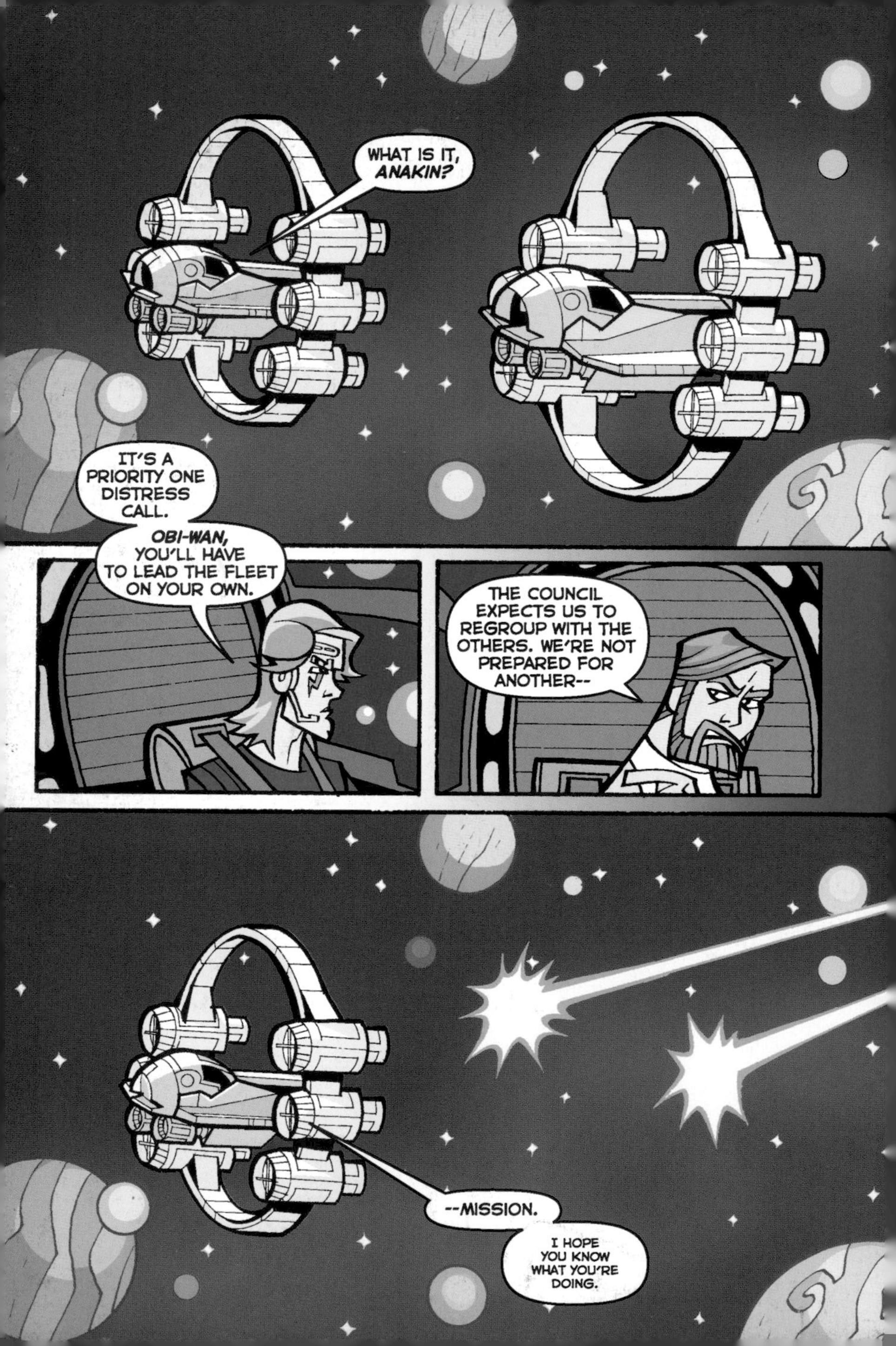
WHAT IS IT, ANAKIN?
IT'S A PRIORITY ONE DISTRESS CALL.
OBI-WAN, YOU'LL HAVE TO LEAD THE FLEET ON YOUR OWN.
THE COUNCIL EXPECTS US TO REGROUP WITH THE OTHERS. WE'RE NOT PREPARED FOR ANOTHER--
--MISSION.
I HOPE YOU KNOW WHAT YOU'RE DOING.

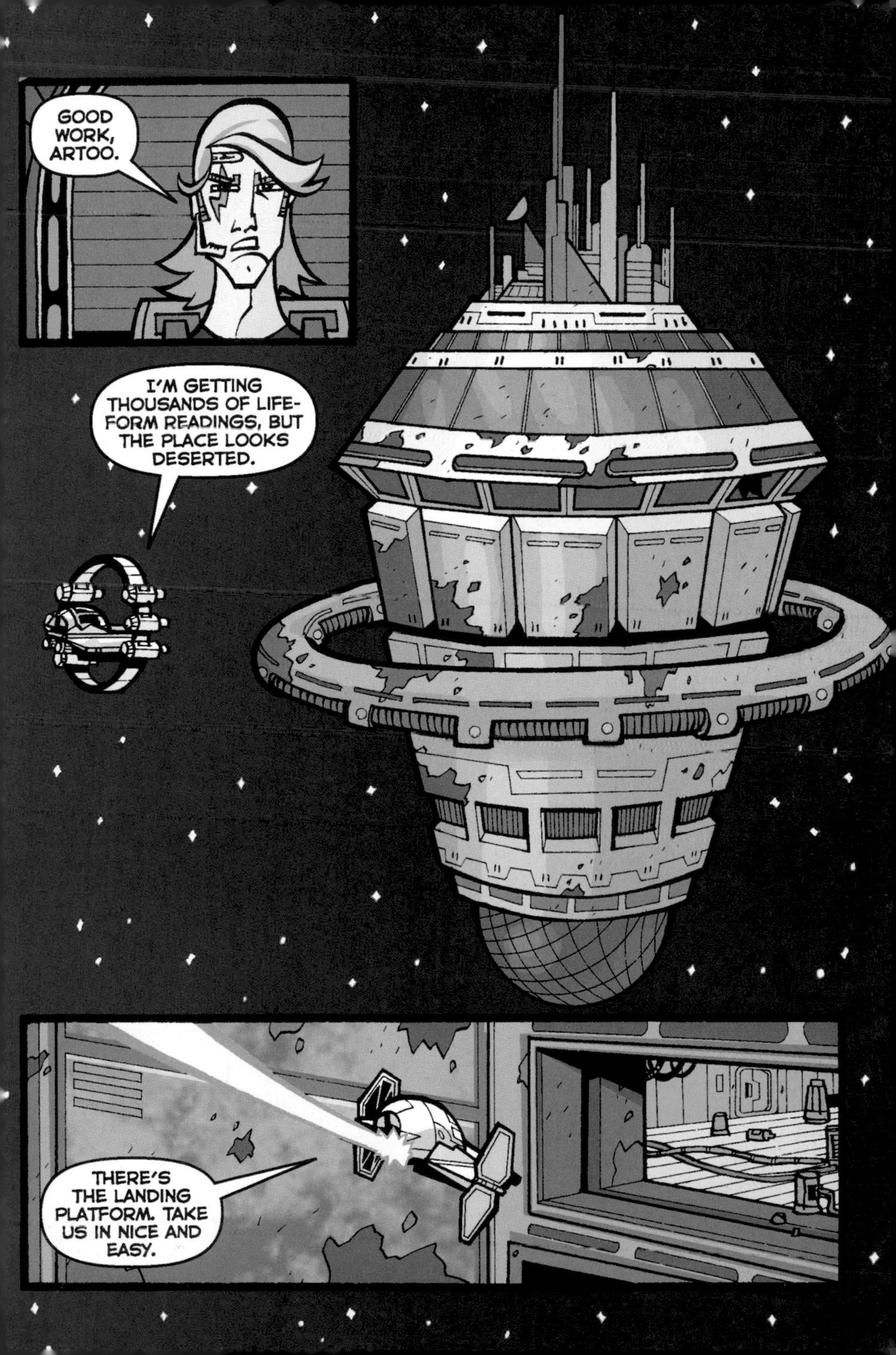
GOOD WORK, ARTOO.
I'M GETTING THOUSANDS OF LIFE-FORM READINGS, BUT THE PLACE LOOKS DESERTED.
THERE'S THE LANDING PLATFORM. TAKE US IN NICE AND EASY.

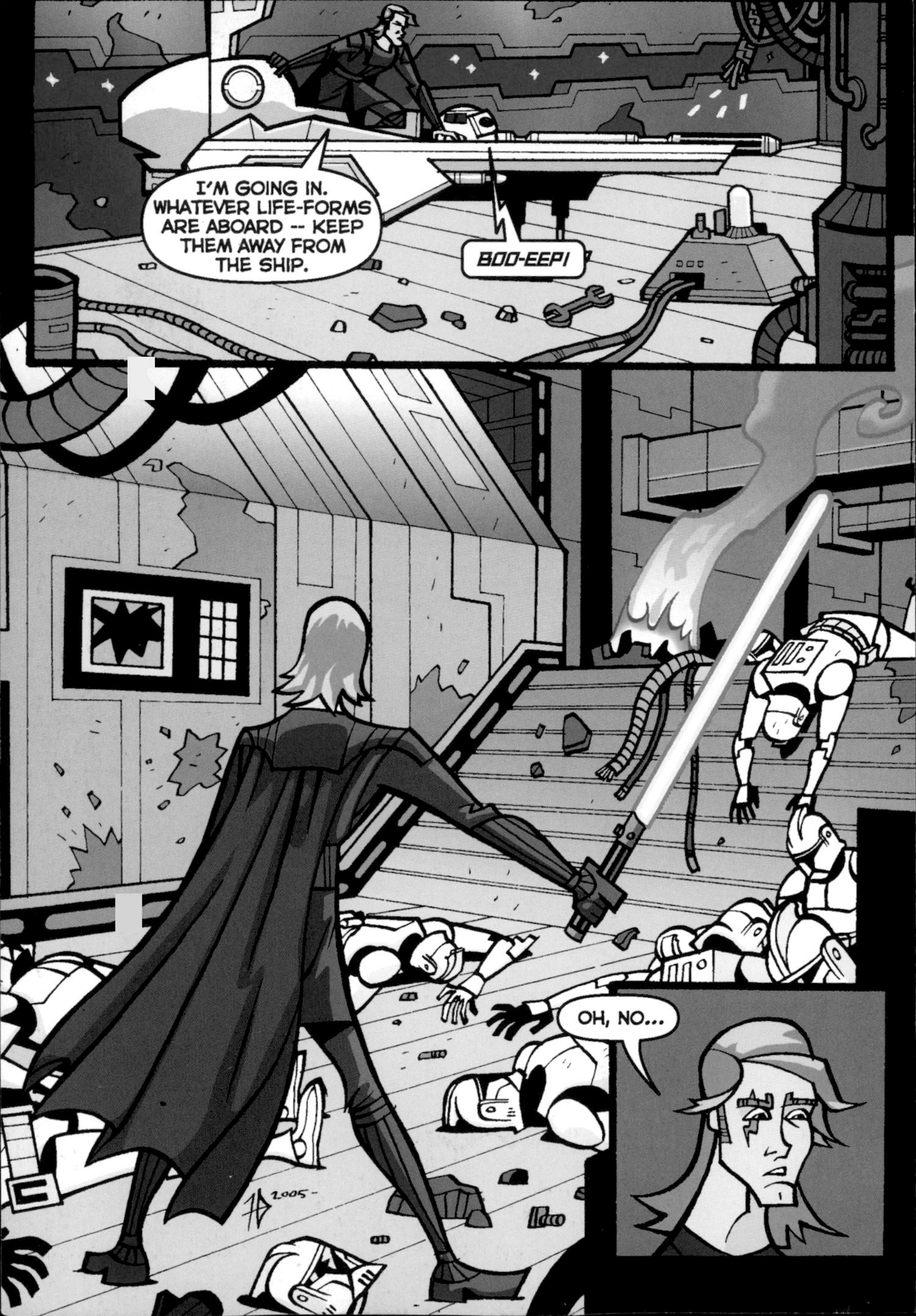
I'M GOING IN. WHATEVER LIFE-FORMS ARE ABOARD -- KEEP THEM AWAY FROM THE SHIP.
BOO-EEP!
OH, NO...

VNNNN!

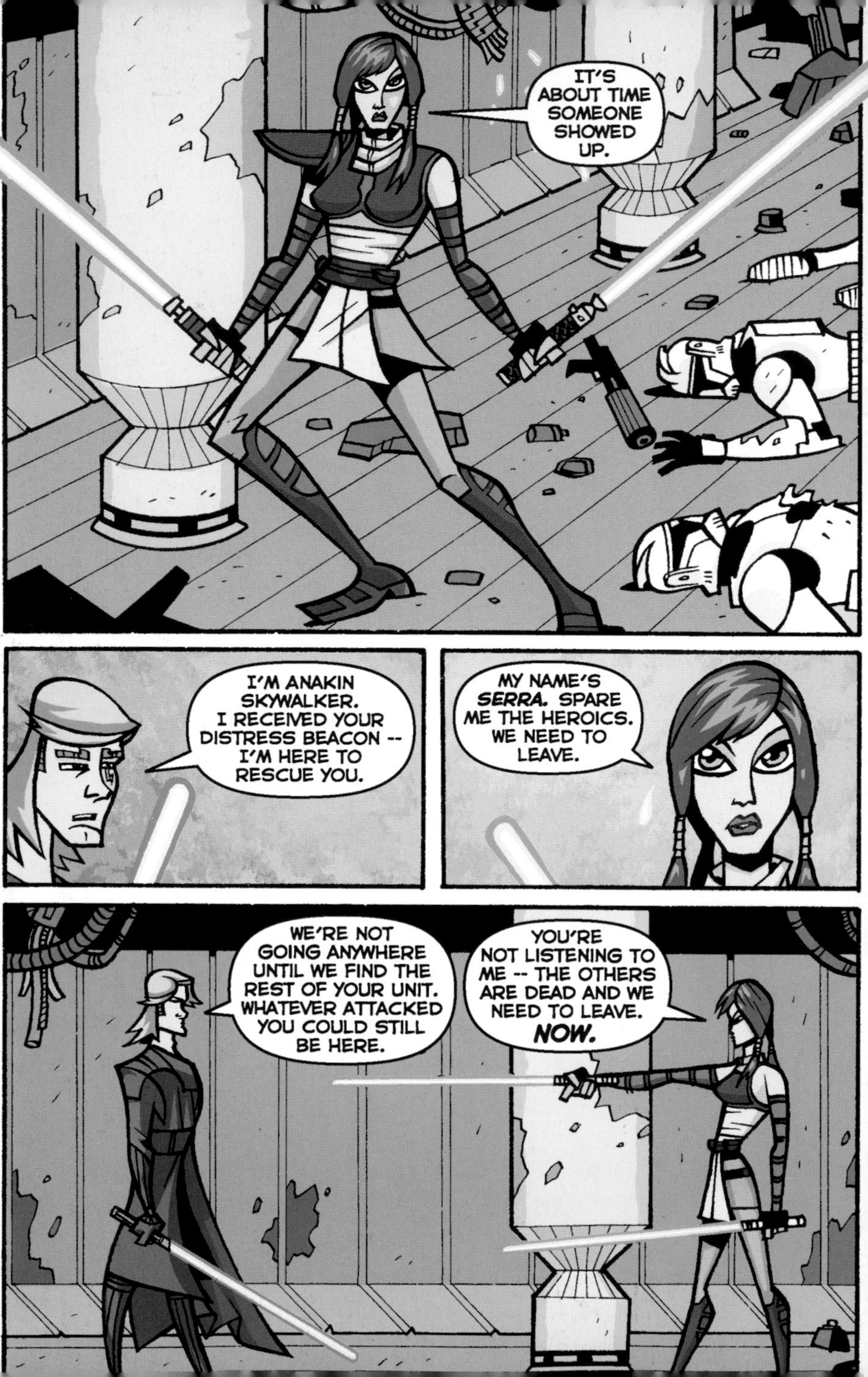
IT'S ABOUT TIME SOMEONE SHOWED UP.
I'M ANAKIN SKYWALKER. I RECEIVED YOUR DISTRESS BEACON -- I'M HERE TO RESCUE YOU.
MY NAME'S *SERRA.* SPARE ME THE HEROICS. WE NEED TO LEAVE.
WE'RE NOT GOING ANYWHERE UNTIL WE FIND THE REST OF YOUR UNIT. WHATEVER ATTACKED YOU COULD STILL BE HERE.
YOU'RE NOT LISTENING TO ME -- THE OTHERS ARE DEAD AND WE NEED TO LEAVE. ***NOW.***

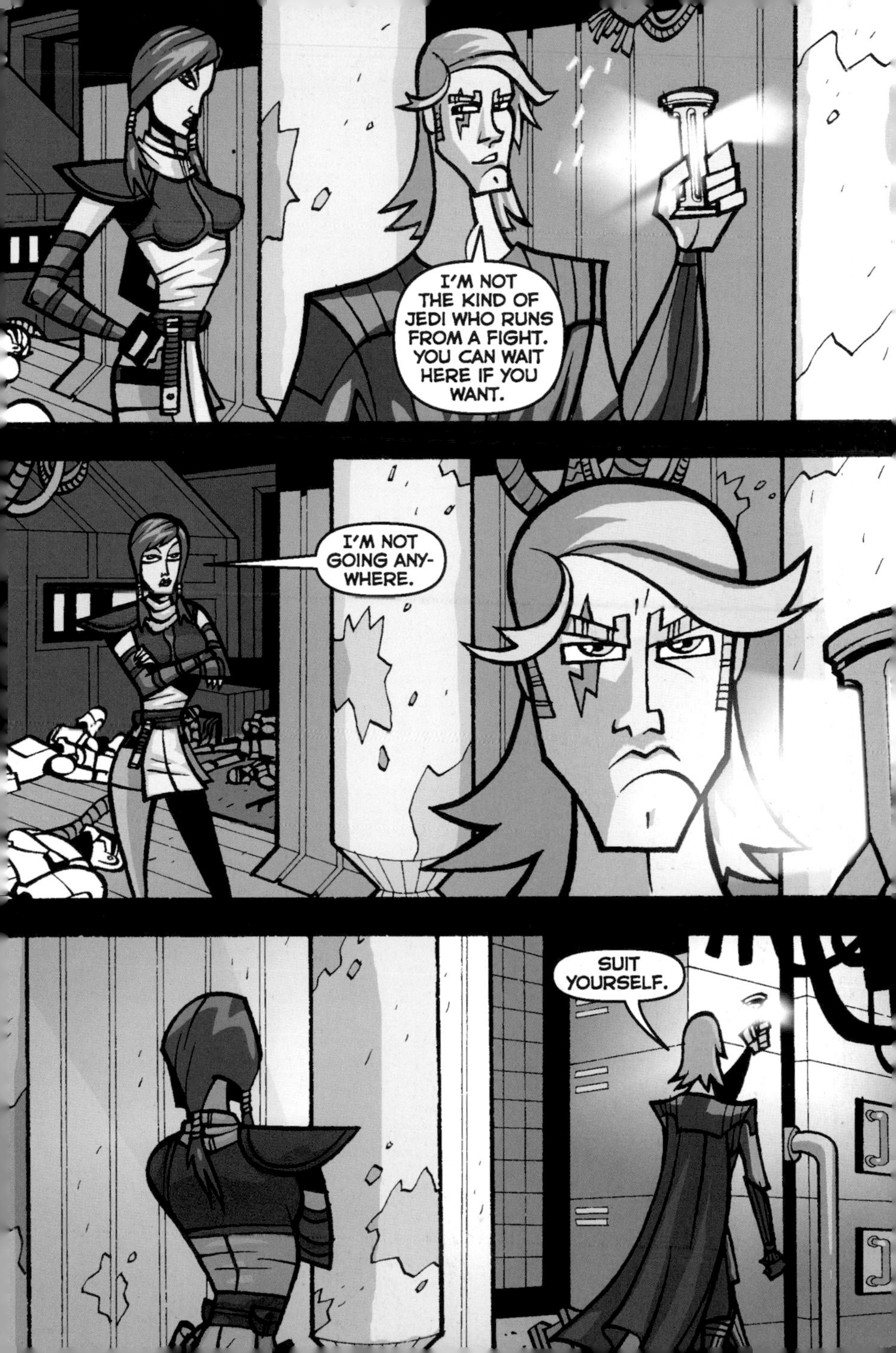
I'M NOT THE KIND OF JEDI WHO RUNS FROM A FIGHT. YOU CAN WAIT HERE IF YOU WANT.
I'M NOT GOING ANY-WHERE.
SUIT YOURSELF.

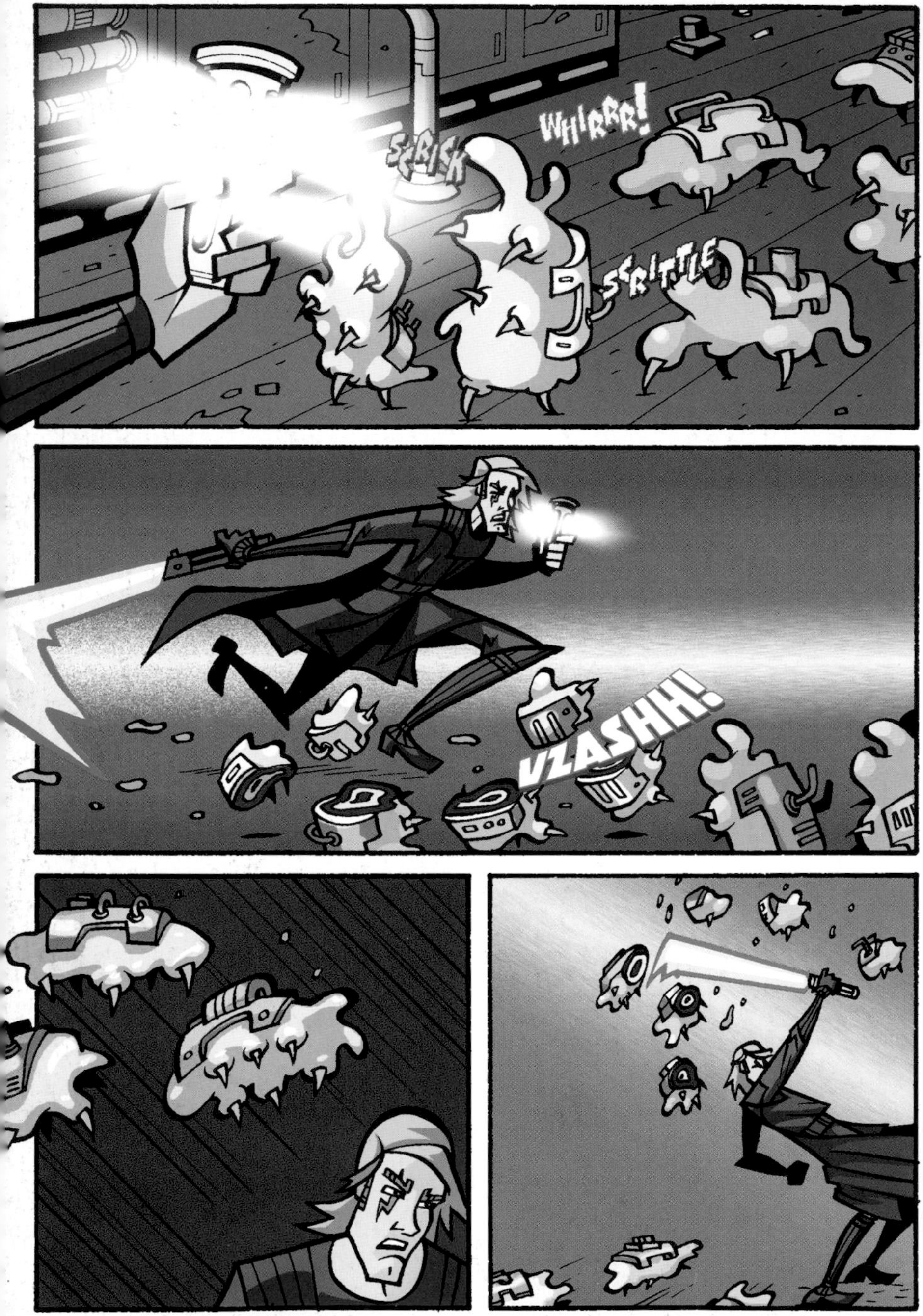
SCRISK
WHIRRR!
SCRITTLE
VZASHH!

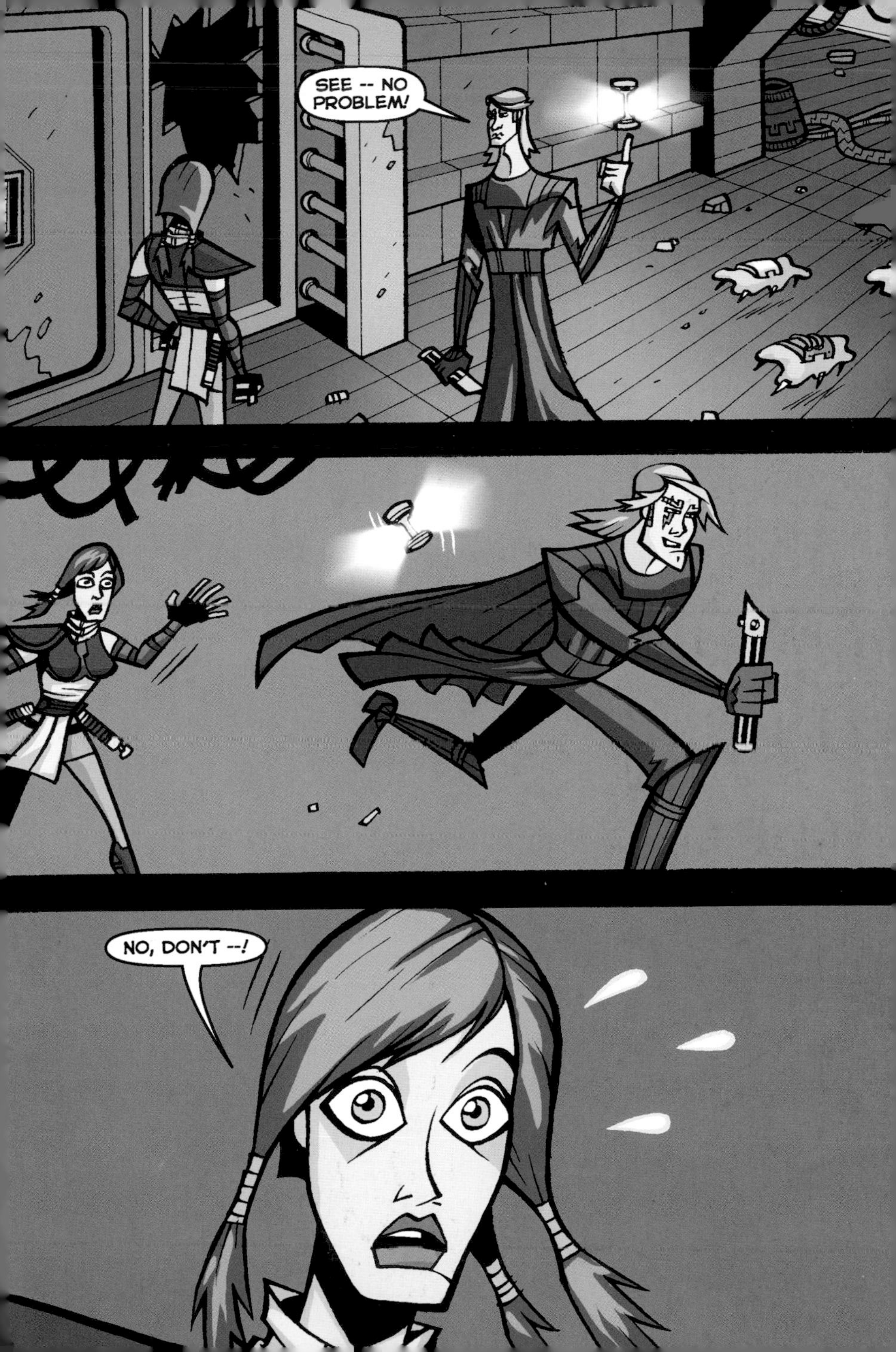
SEE -- NO PROBLEM!
NO, DON'T --!

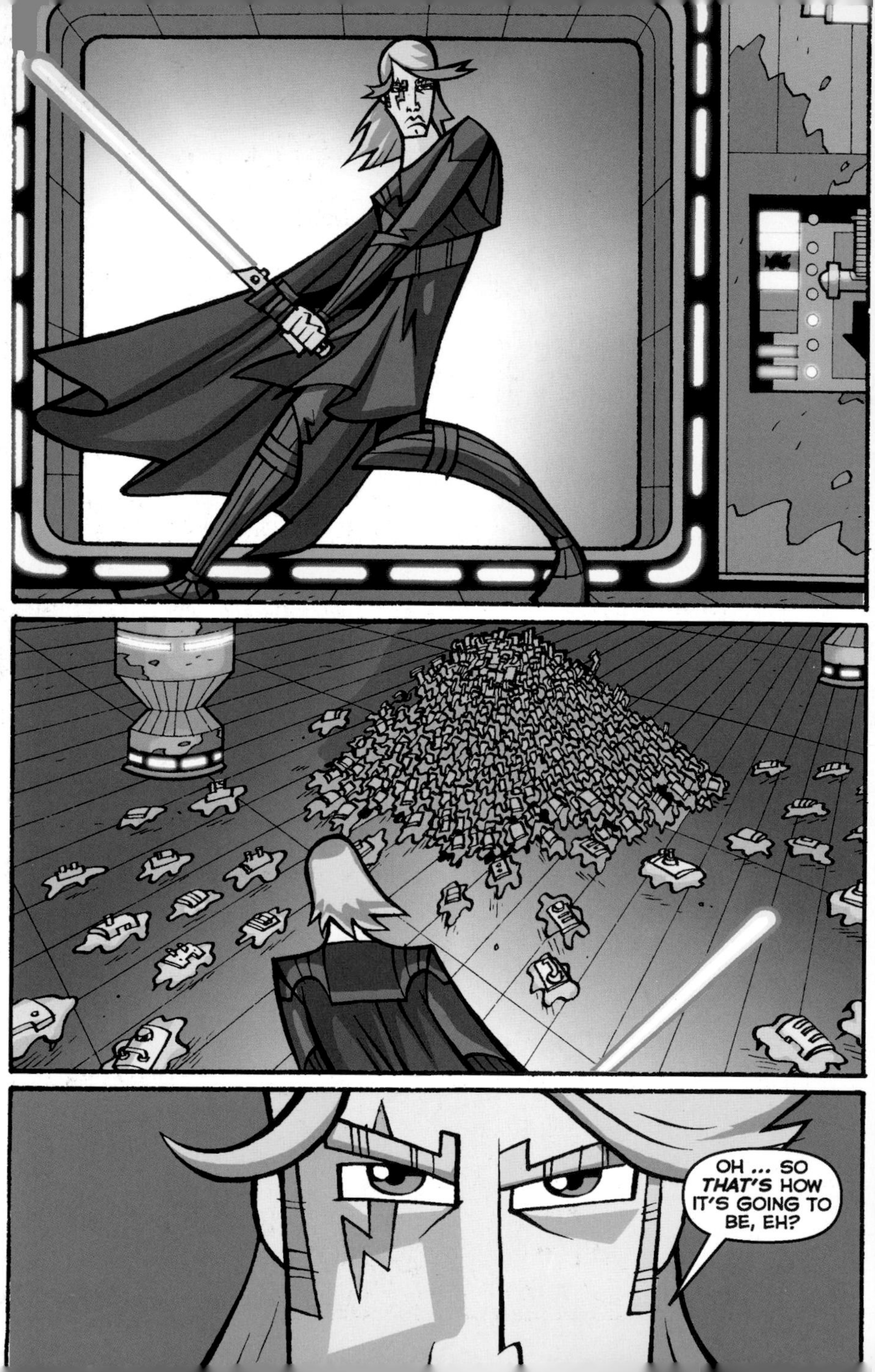
OH ... SO *THAT'S* HOW IT'S GOING TO BE, EH?

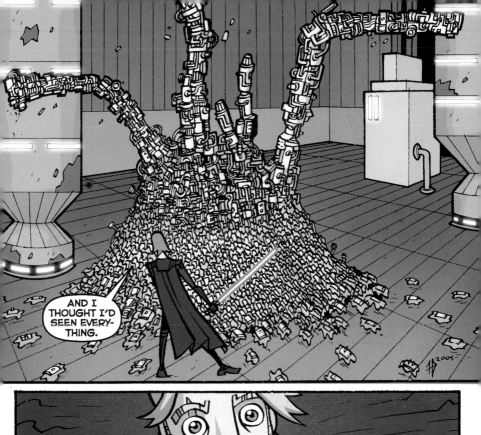

AND I THOUGHT I'D SEEN EVERY-THING.

KRA-KOOM!

VVZZMM!

I COULD USE SOME HELP HERE!

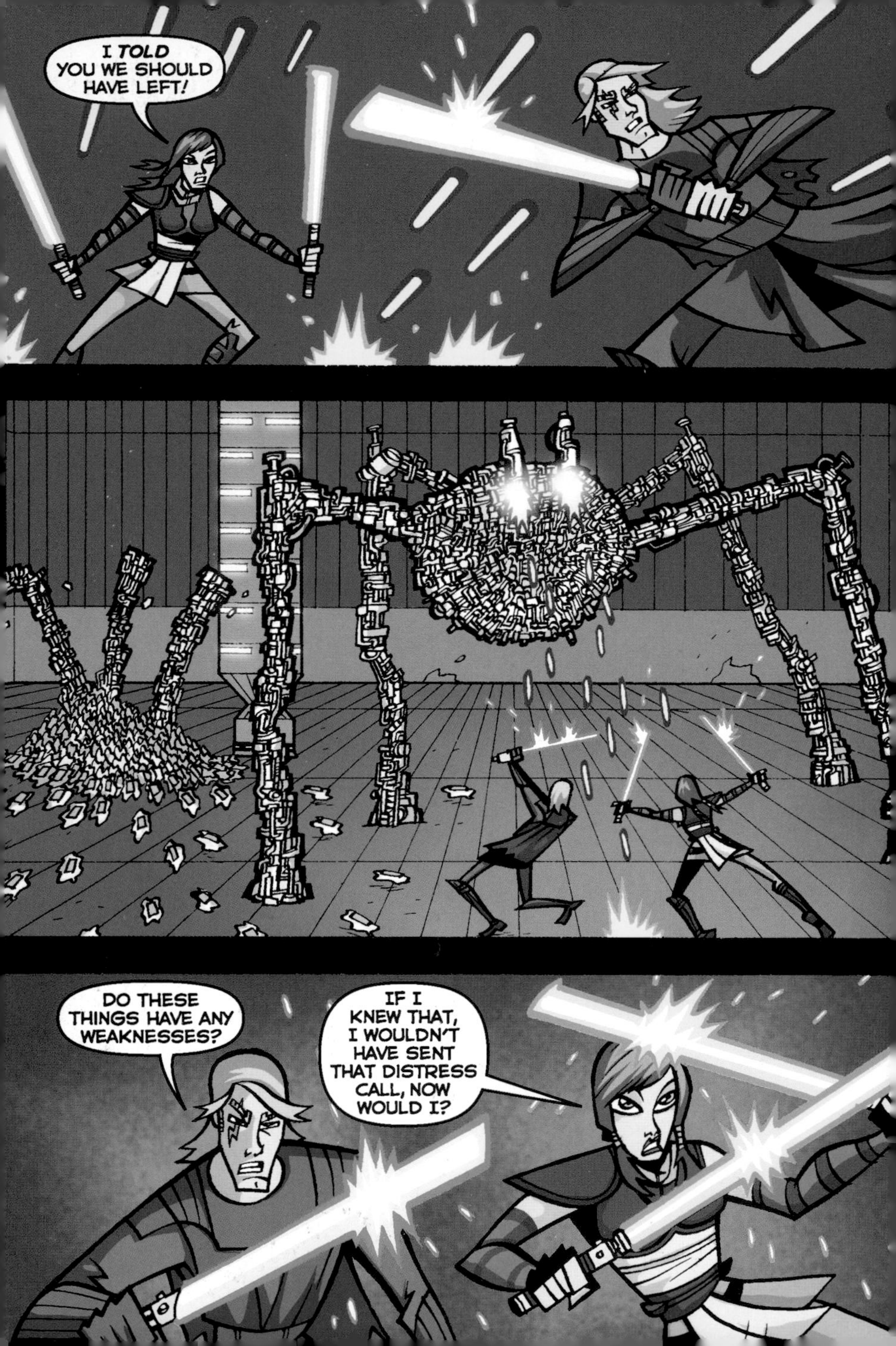
I *TOLD* YOU WE SHOULD HAVE LEFT!
DO THESE THINGS HAVE ANY WEAKNESSES?
IF I KNEW THAT, I WOULDN'T HAVE SENT THAT DISTRESS CALL, NOW WOULD I?

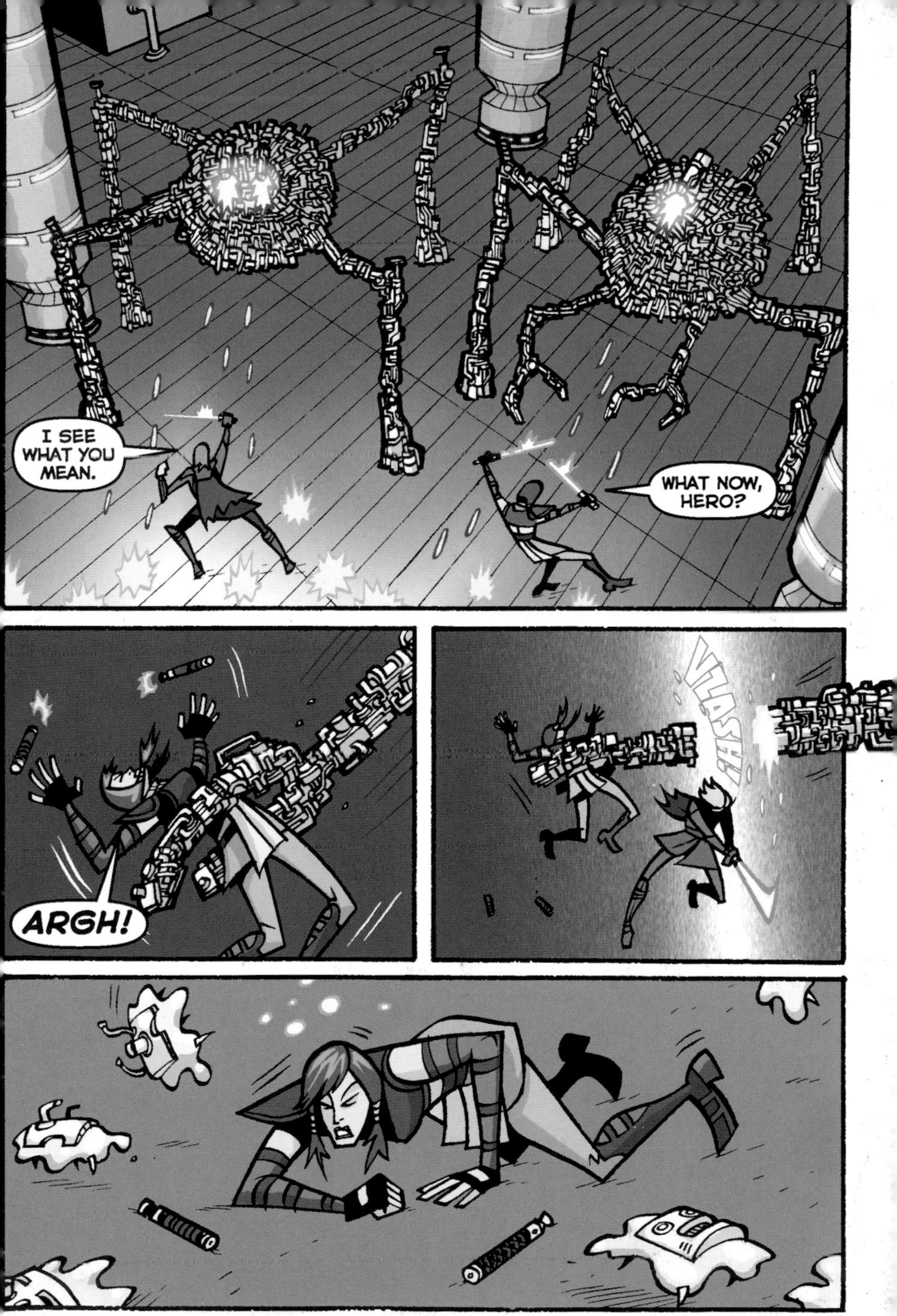
I SEE WHAT YOU MEAN.
WHAT NOW, HERO?
ARGH!
VZASH!

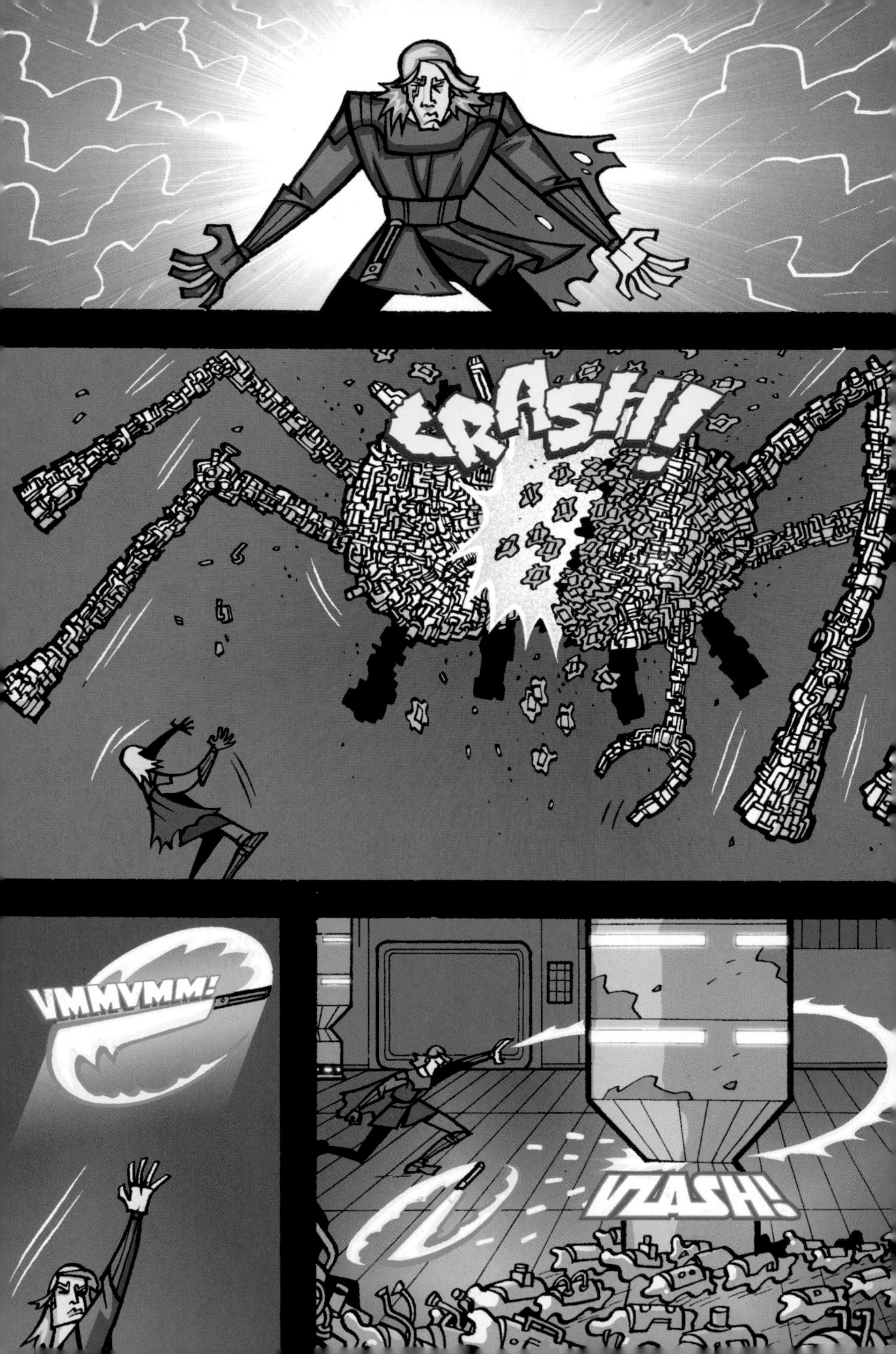
CRASH!
VMMVMM!
VZASH!

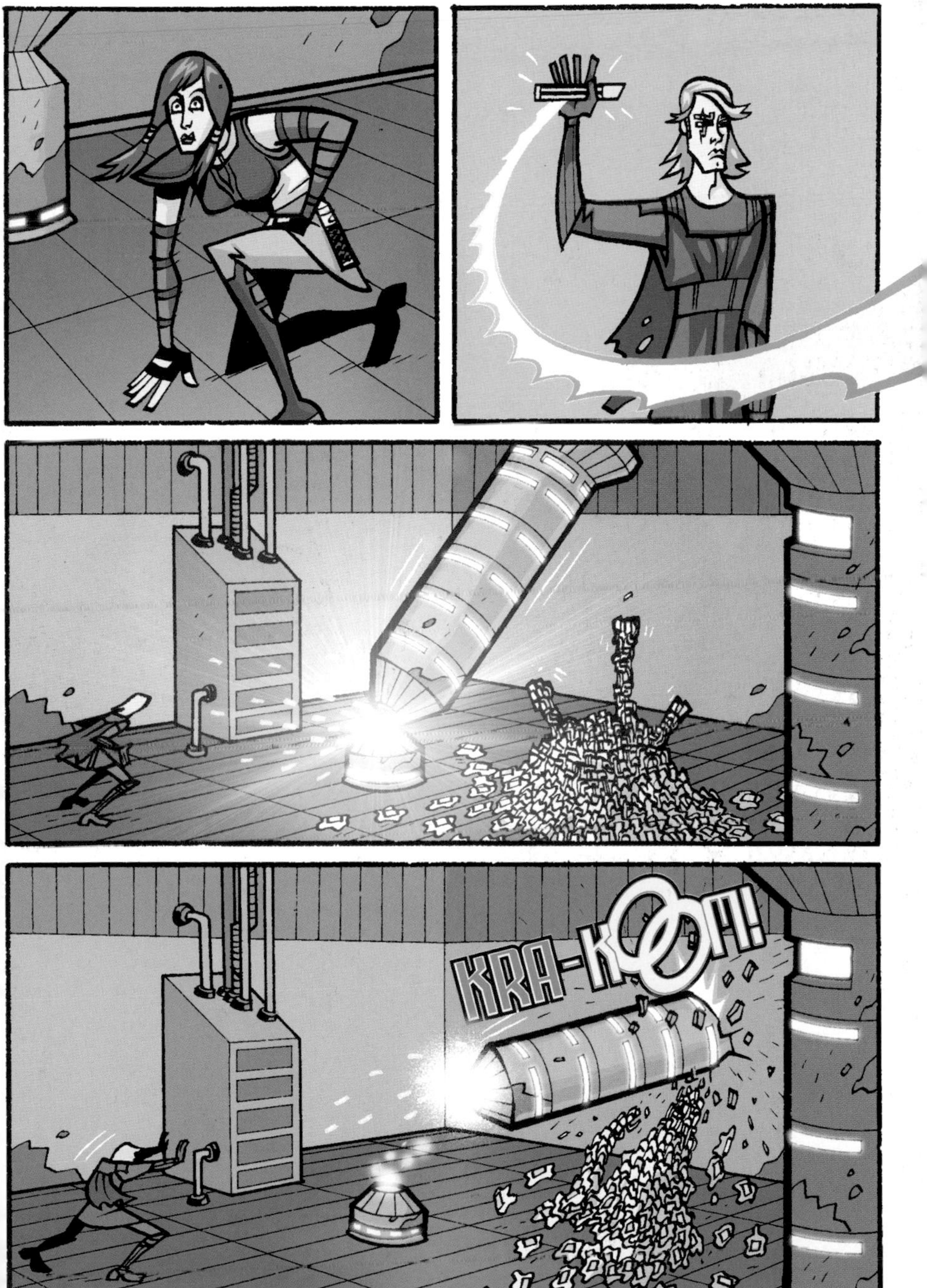
KRA-KOOM!

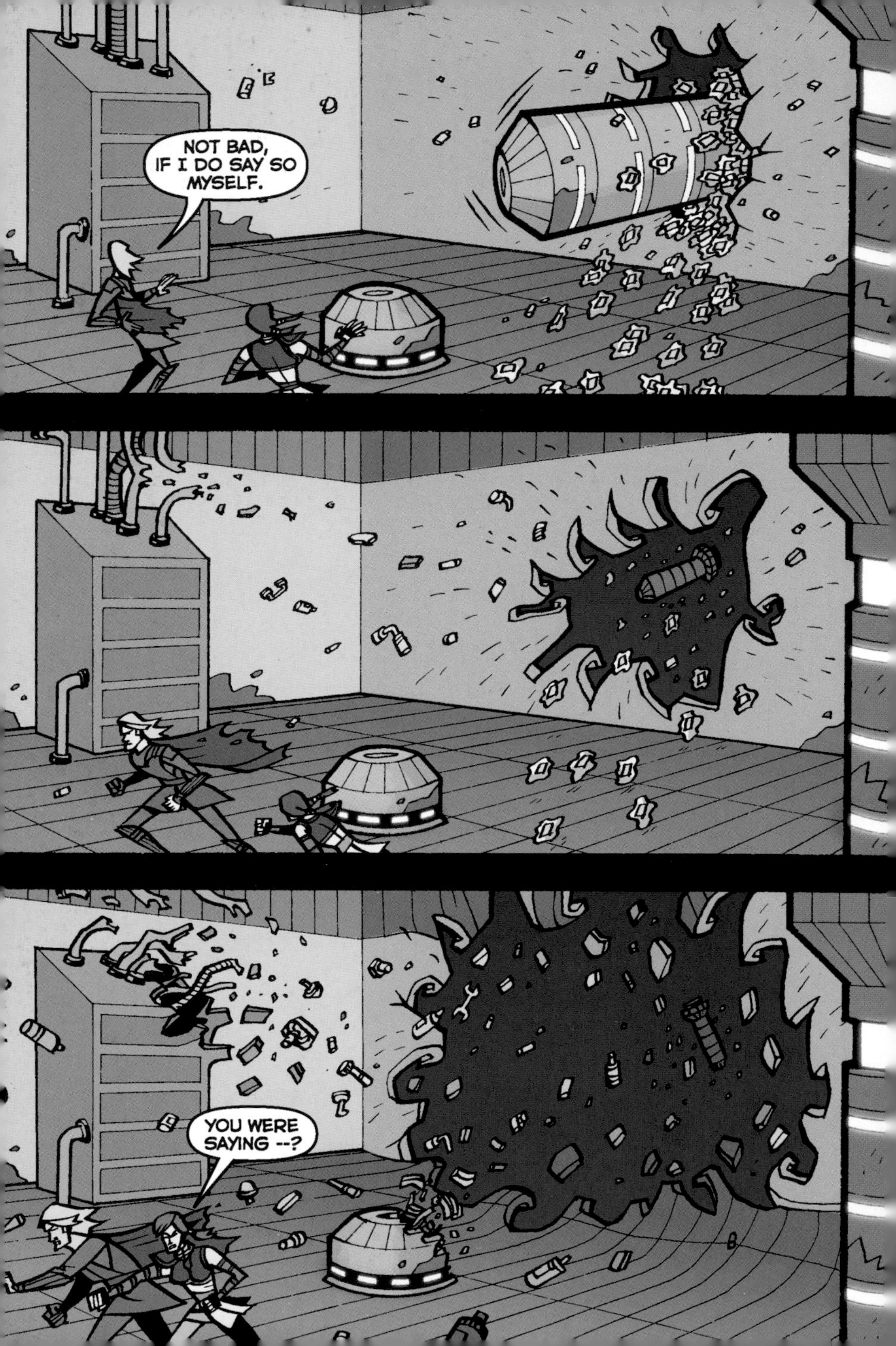
NOT BAD, IF I DO SAY SO MYSELF.
YOU WERE SAYING --?

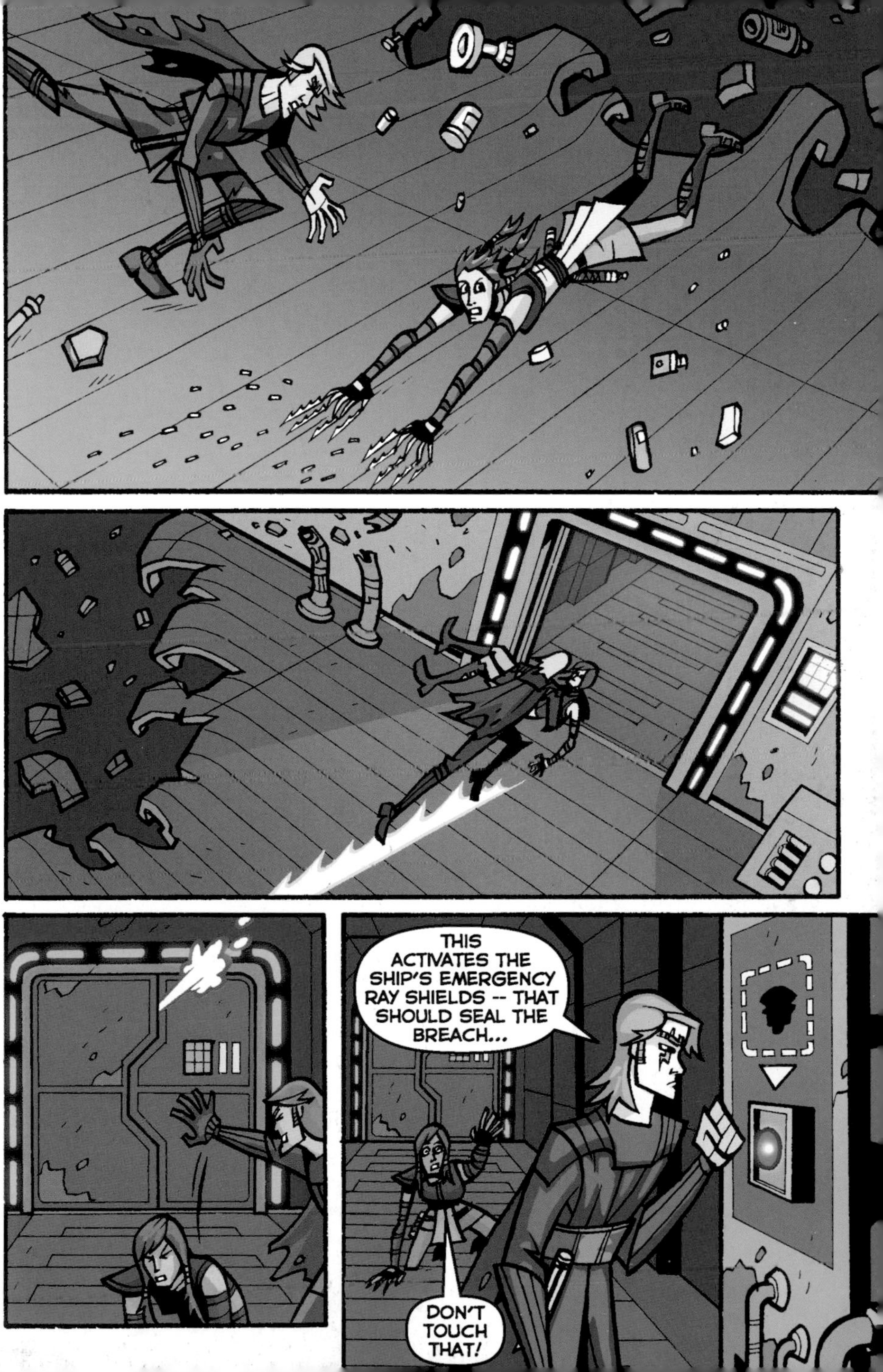
THIS ACTIVATES THE SHIP'S EMERGENCY RAY SHIELDS -- THAT SHOULD SEAL THE BREACH...
DON'T TOUCH THAT!

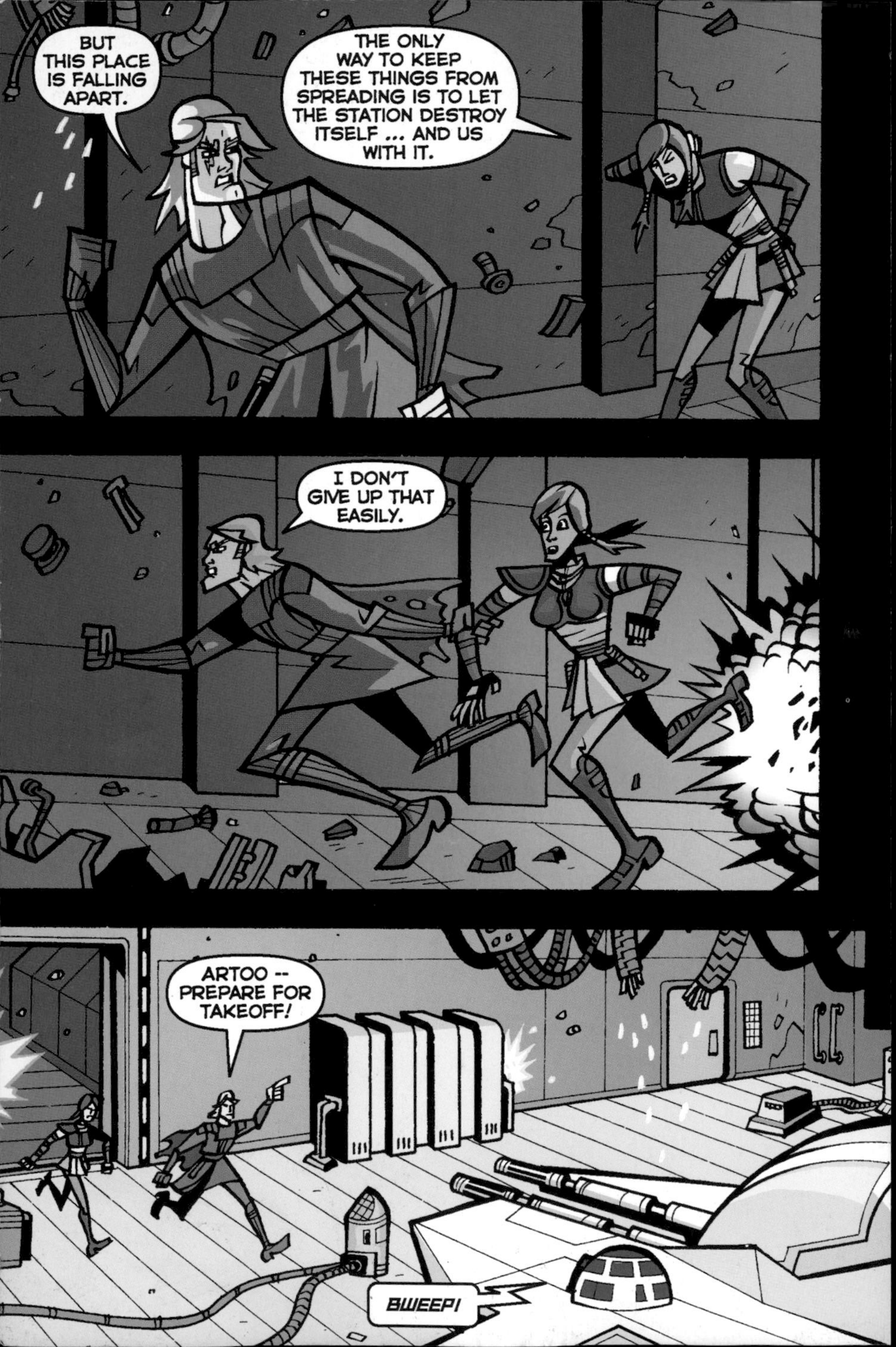
BUT THIS PLACE IS FALLING APART.
THE ONLY WAY TO KEEP THESE THINGS FROM SPREADING IS TO LET THE STATION DESTROY ITSELF ... AND US WITH IT.
I DON'T GIVE UP THAT EASILY.
ARTOO -- PREPARE FOR TAKEOFF!
BWEEP!

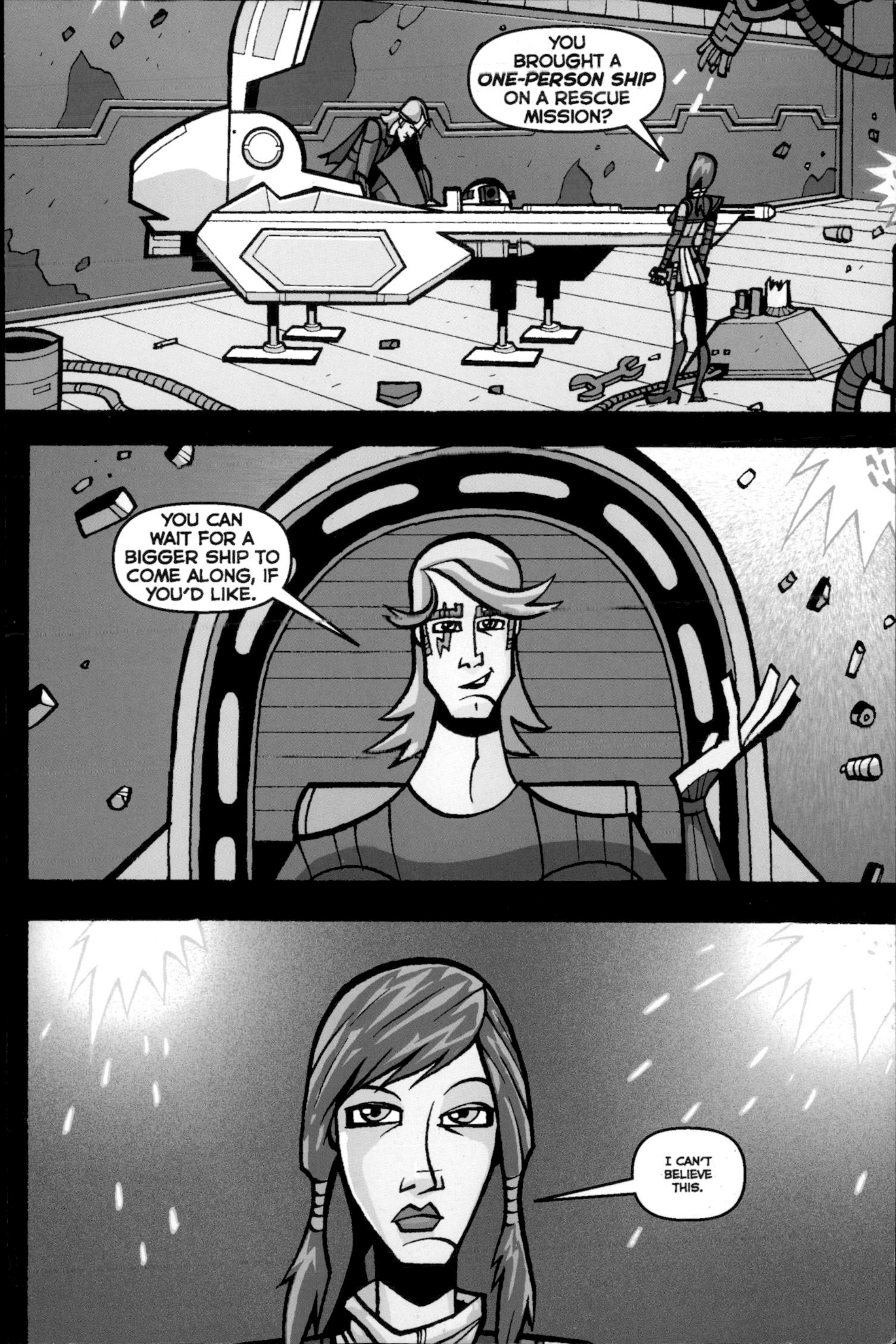
YOU BROUGHT A *ONE-PERSON SHIP* ON A RESCUE MISSION?
YOU CAN WAIT FOR A BIGGER SHIP TO COME ALONG, IF YOU'D LIKE.
I CAN'T BELIEVE THIS.

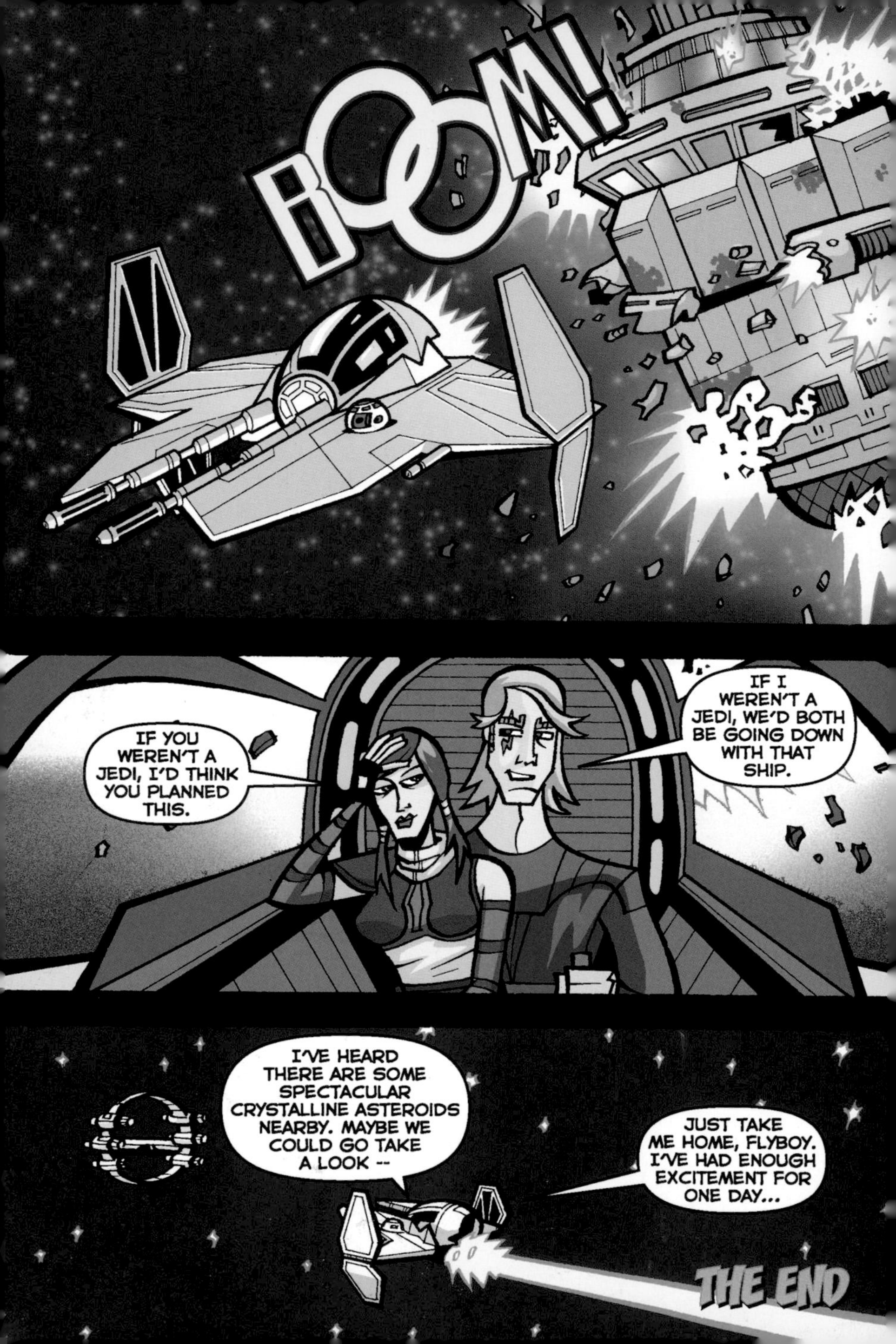
BOOM!
IF YOU WEREN'T A JEDI, I'D THINK YOU PLANNED THIS.
IF I WEREN'T A JEDI, WE'D BOTH BE GOING DOWN WITH THAT SHIP.
I'VE HEARD THERE ARE SOME SPECTACULAR CRYSTALLINE ASTEROIDS NEARBY. MAYBE WE COULD GO TAKE A LOOK --
JUST TAKE ME HOME, FLYBOY. I'VE HAD ENOUGH EXCITEMENT FOR ONE DAY...
THE END

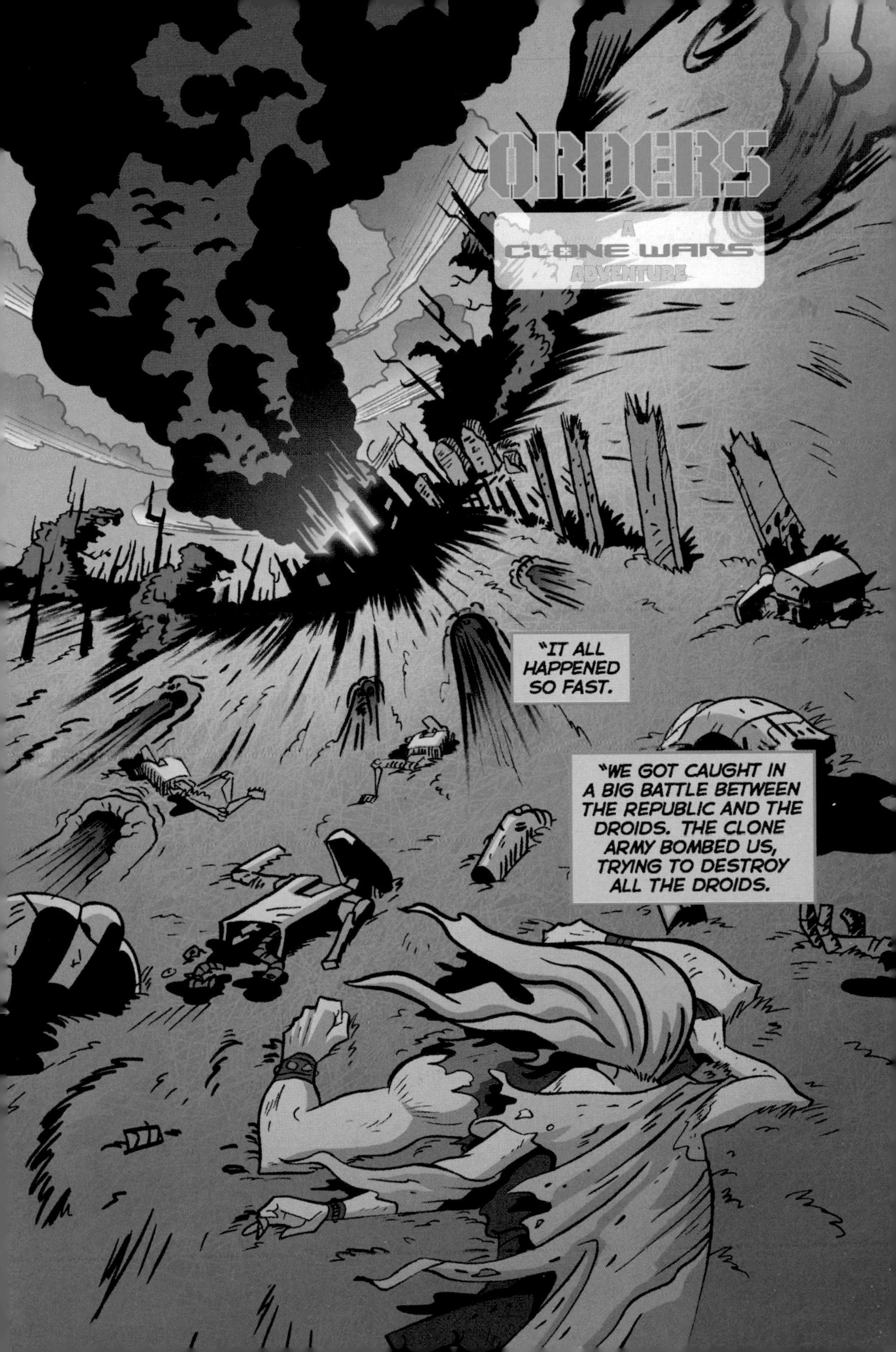
ORDERS
A
CLONE WARS
ADVENTURE
"IT ALL HAPPENED SO FAST.
"WE GOT CAUGHT IN A BIG BATTLE BETWEEN THE REPUBLIC AND THE DROIDS. THE CLONE ARMY BOMBED US, TRYING TO DESTROY ALL THE DROIDS.

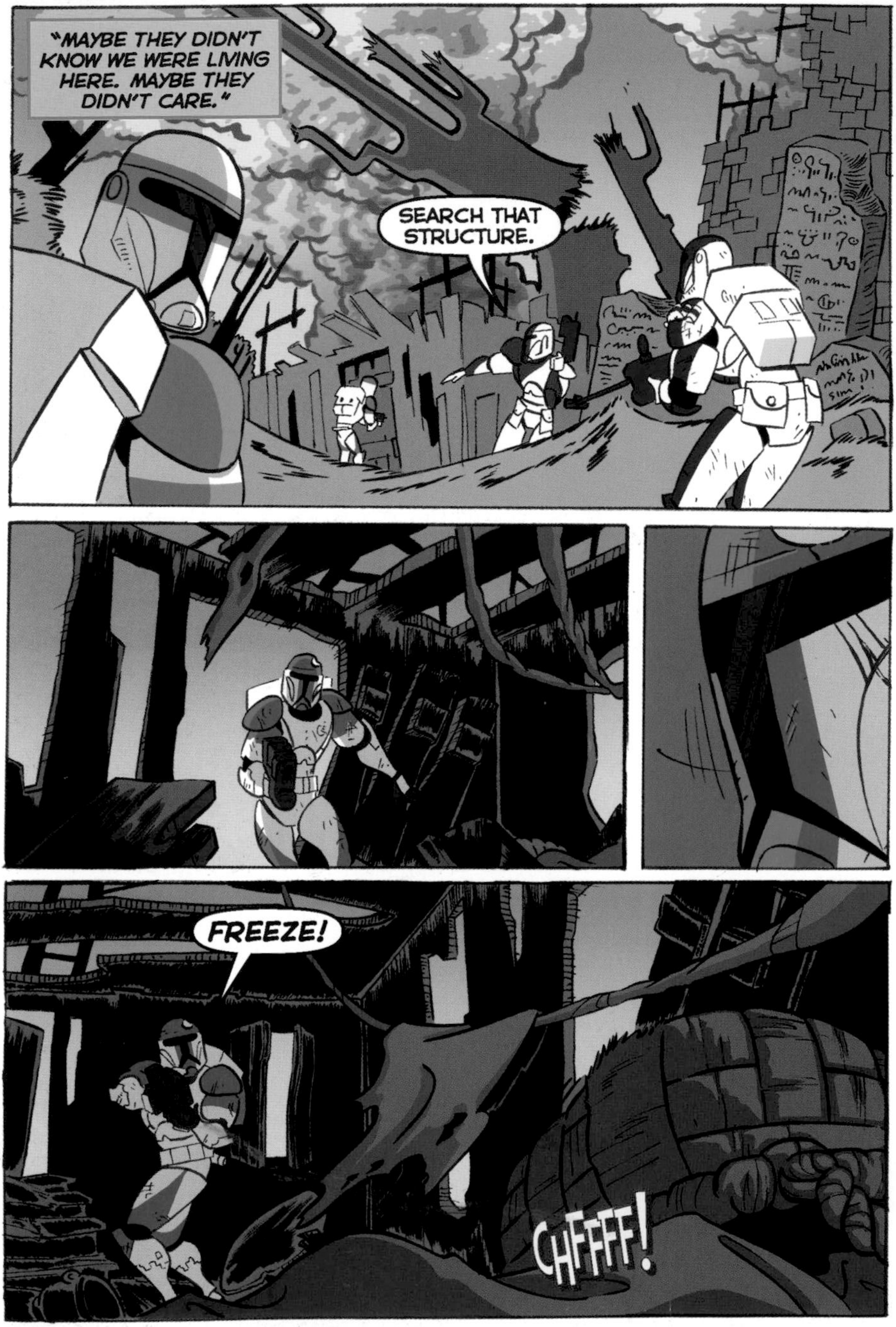
"MAYBE THEY DIDN'T KNOW WE WERE LIVING HERE. MAYBE THEY DIDN'T CARE."
SEARCH THAT STRUCTURE.
FREEZE!
CHFFFF!

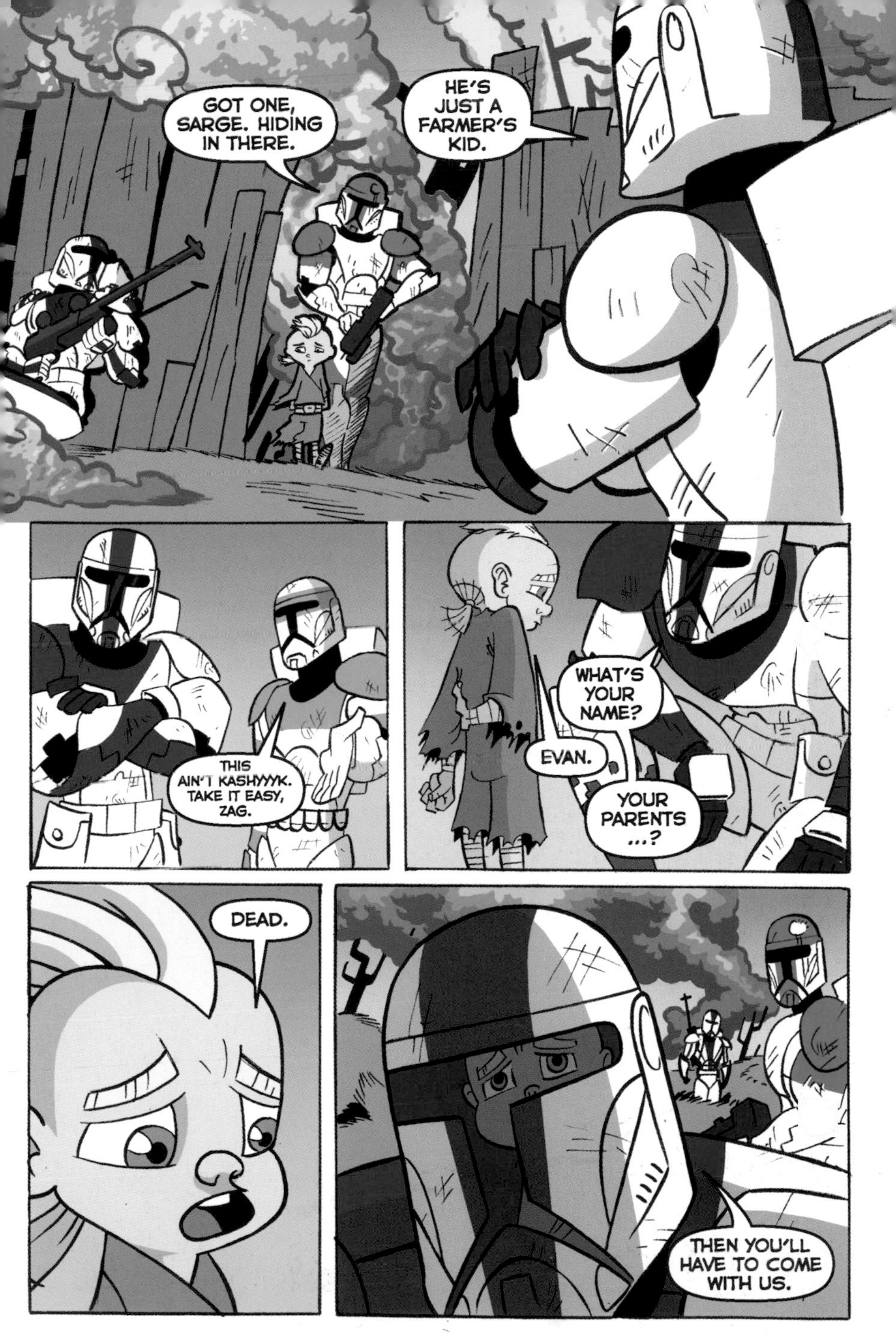
GOT ONE, SARGE. HIDING IN THERE.
HE'S JUST A FARMER'S KID.
THIS AIN'T KASHYYYK. TAKE IT EASY, ZAG.
WHAT'S YOUR NAME?
EVAN.
YOUR PARENTS ...?
DEAD.
THEN YOU'LL HAVE TO COME WITH US.

THOSE ARE OUR ORDERS.
BUT THIS IS MY HOME!
WE'RE TAKING ALL CIVILIANS TO A REFUGEE CAMP ABOUT TWENTY KLICKS FROM HERE.
BUT WHY? WHY DO I HAVE TO GO?
LISTEN VERY CLOSELY TO ME--WE DON'T *QUESTION* ORDERS, WE *FOLLOW* THEM. NOW...WALK.

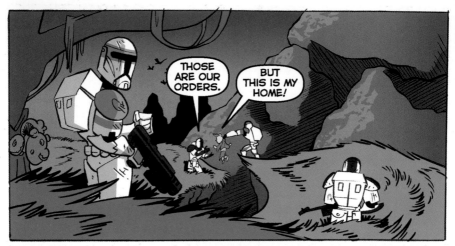

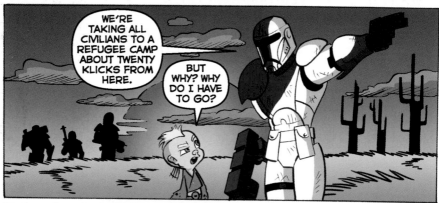

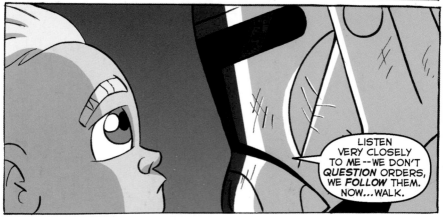

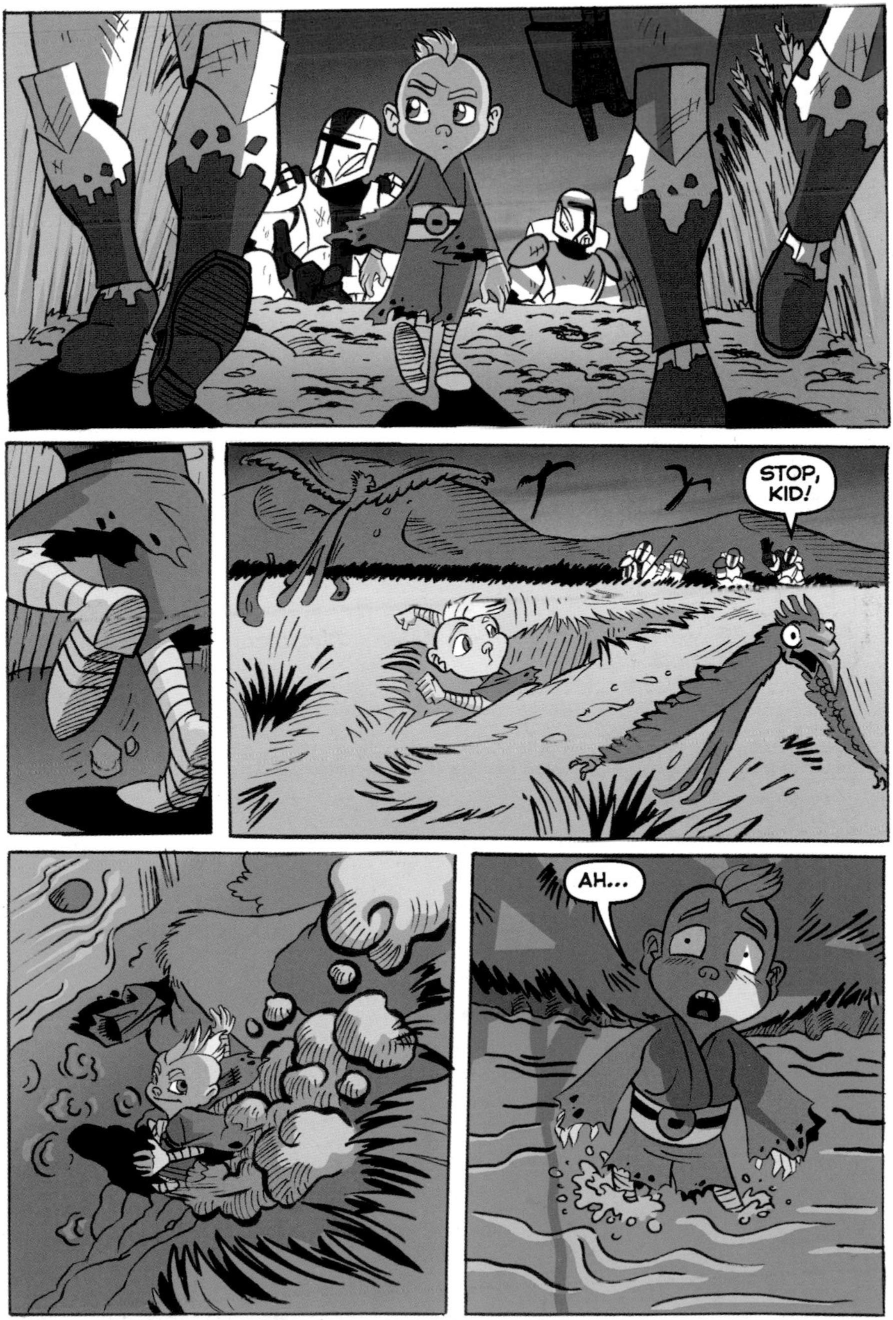
STOP, KID!
AH...

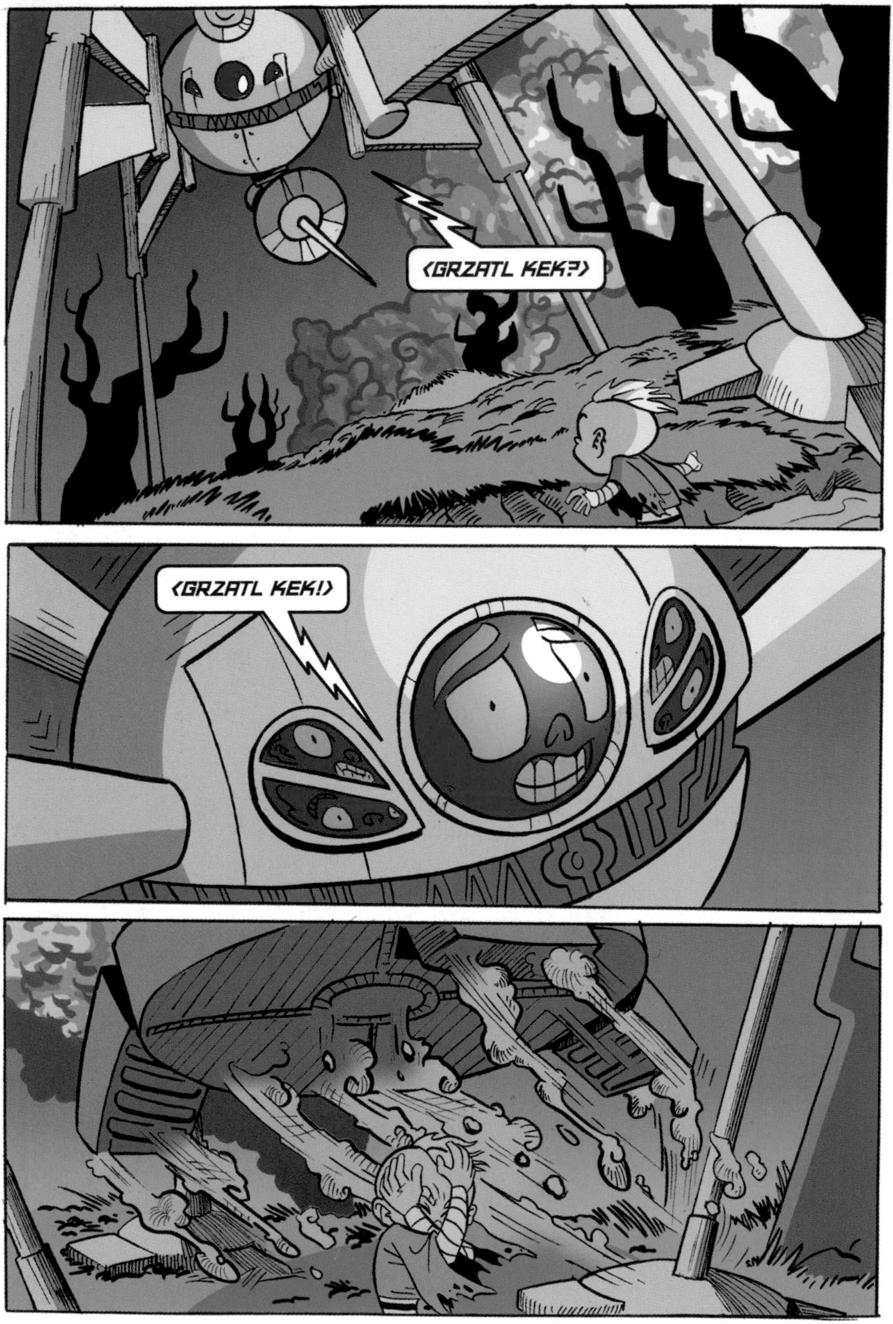
<GRZATL KEK?>
<GRZATL KEK!>

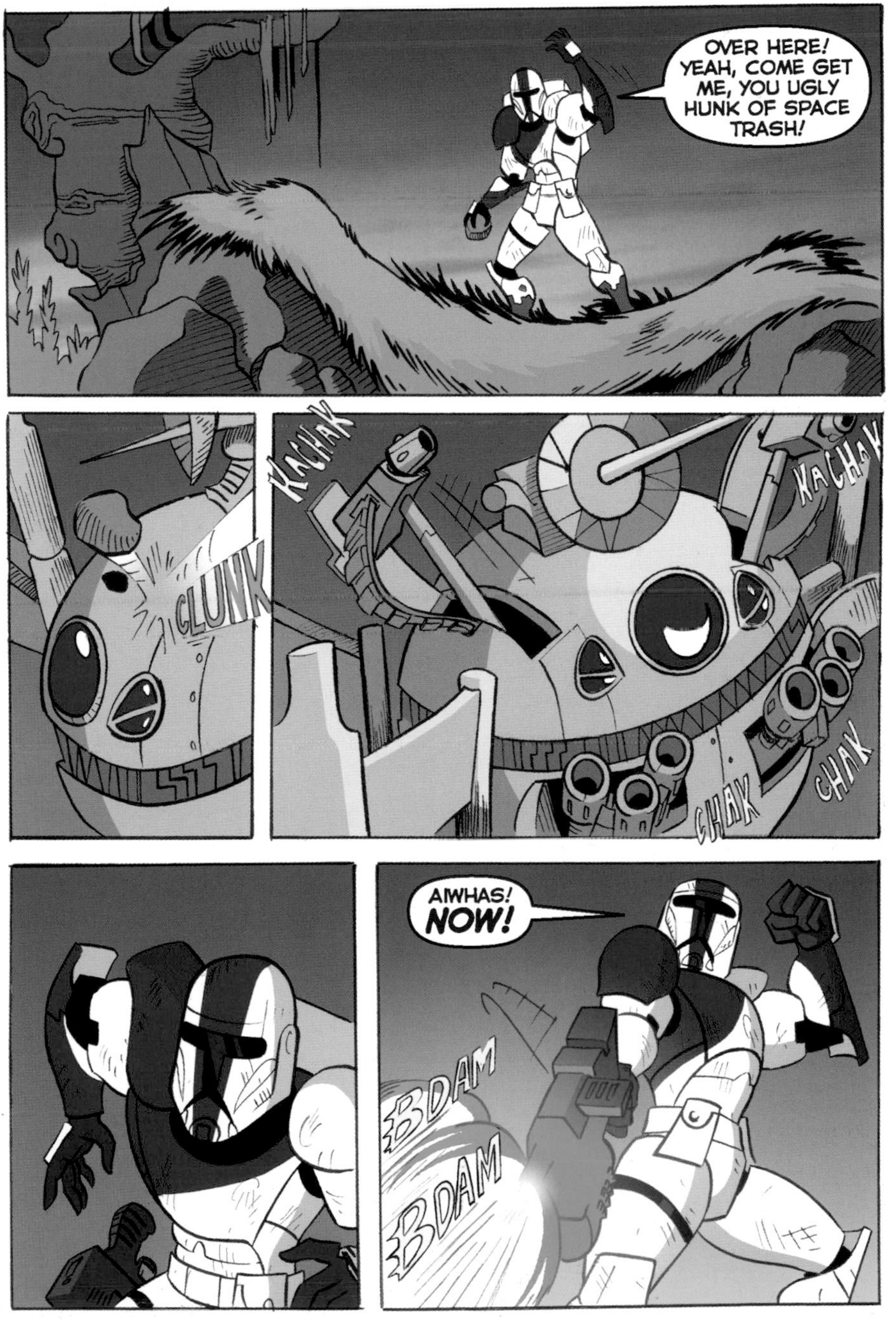

OVER HERE! YEAH, COME GET ME, YOU UGLY HUNK OF SPACE TRASH!
CLUNK
KACHAK
KACHAK
CHAK
CHAK
AIWHAS! NOW!
BDAM
BDAM

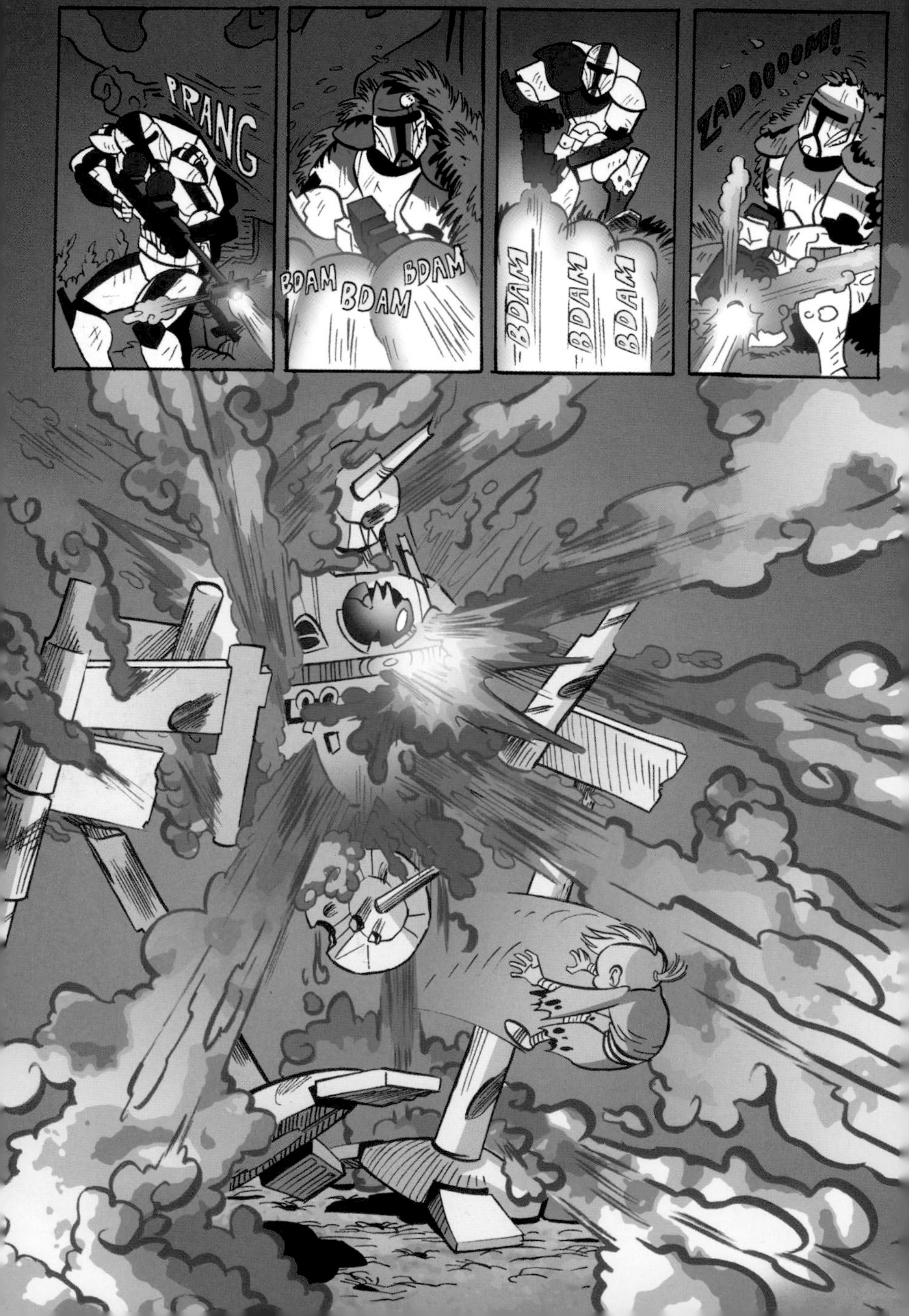
PRANG
BDAM
BDAM
BDAM
BDAM
BDAM
BDAM
ZADOOOOOM!!

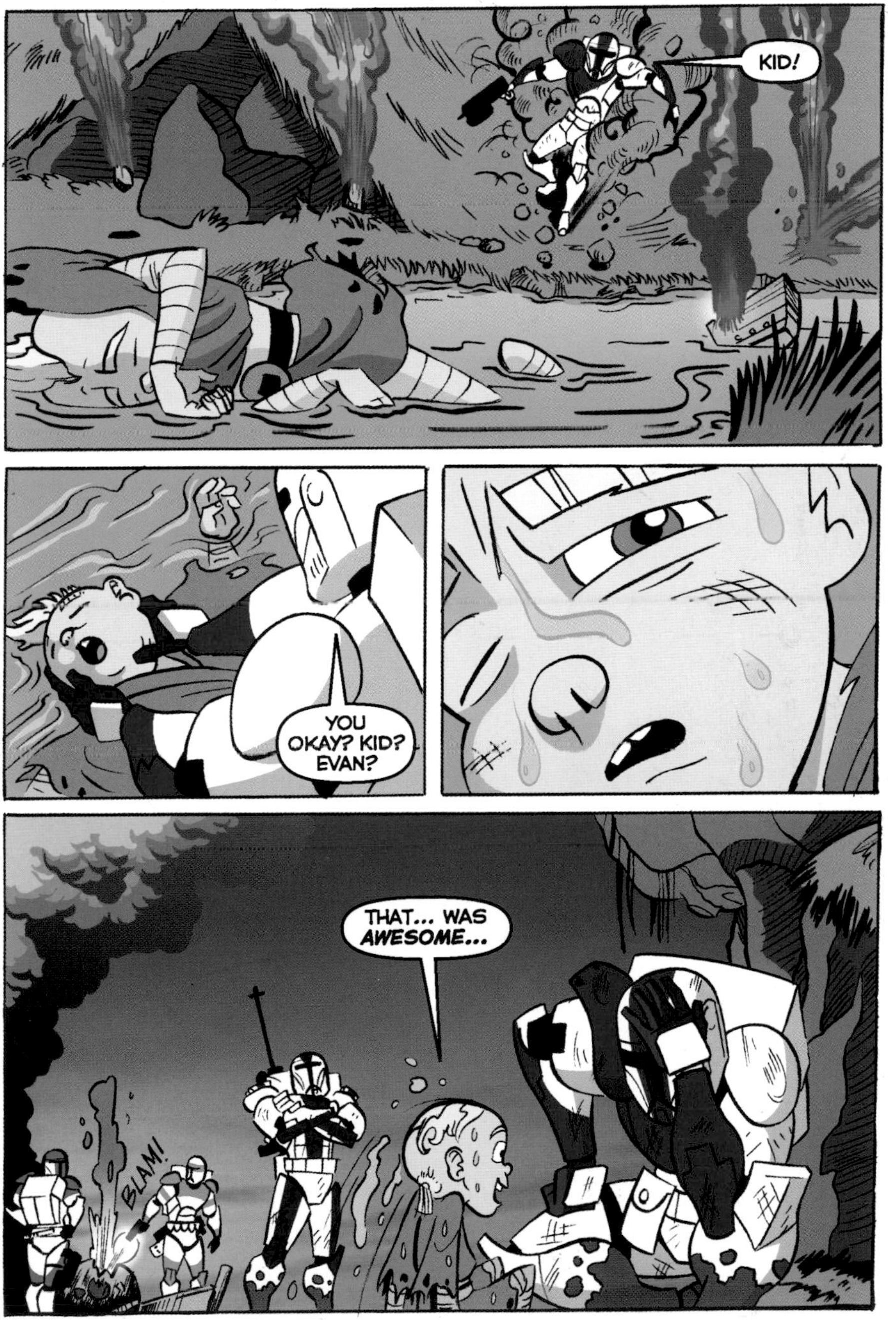
KID!
YOU OKAY? KID? EVAN?
THAT... WAS AWESOME...
BLAM!

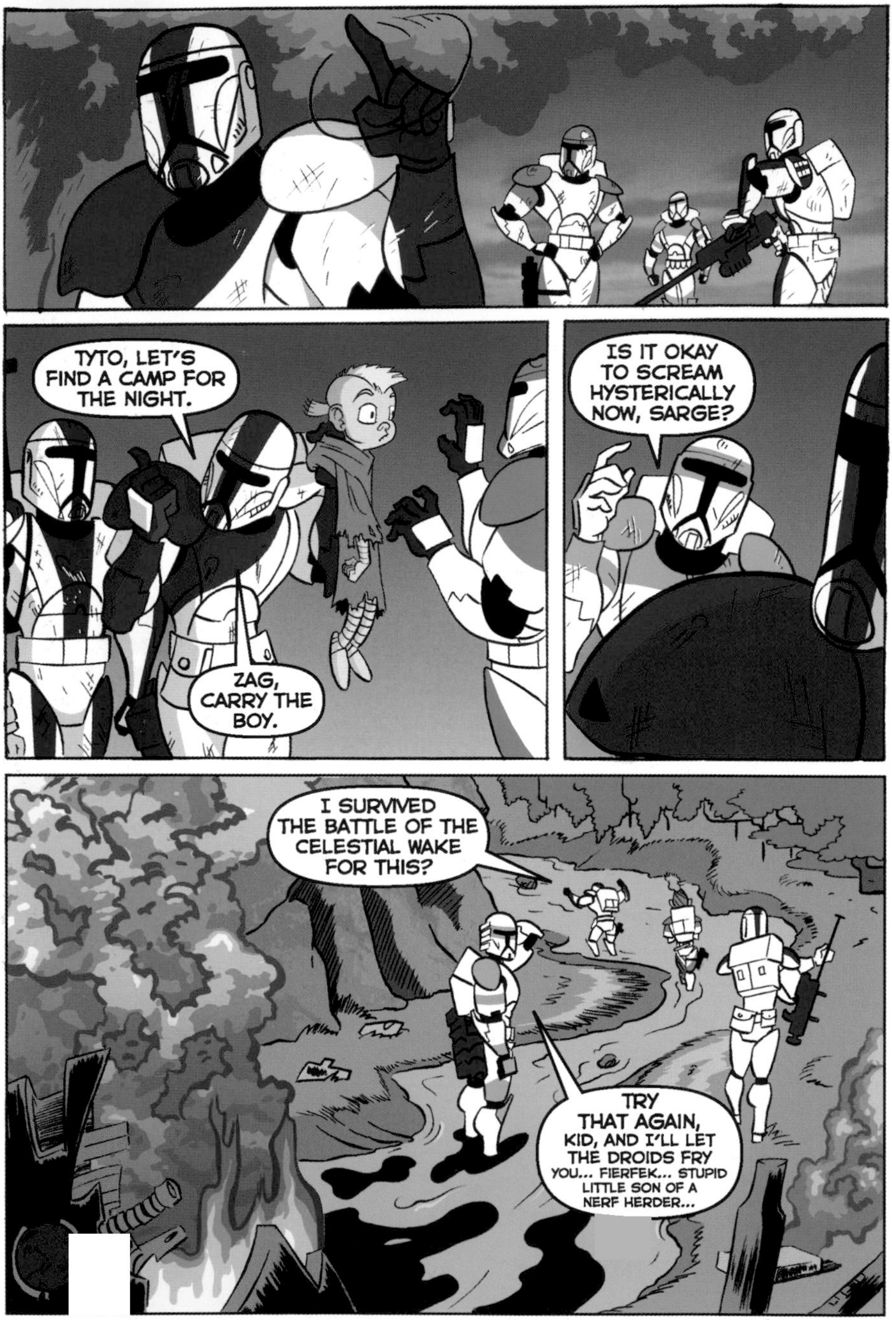
TYTO, LET'S FIND A CAMP FOR THE NIGHT.
ZAG, CARRY THE BOY.
IS IT OKAY TO SCREAM HYSTERICALLY NOW, SARGE?
I SURVIVED THE BATTLE OF THE CELESTIAL WAKE FOR THIS?
TRY THAT AGAIN, KID, AND I'LL LET THE DROIDS FRY YOU... FIERFEK... STUPID LITTLE SON OF A NERF HERDER...

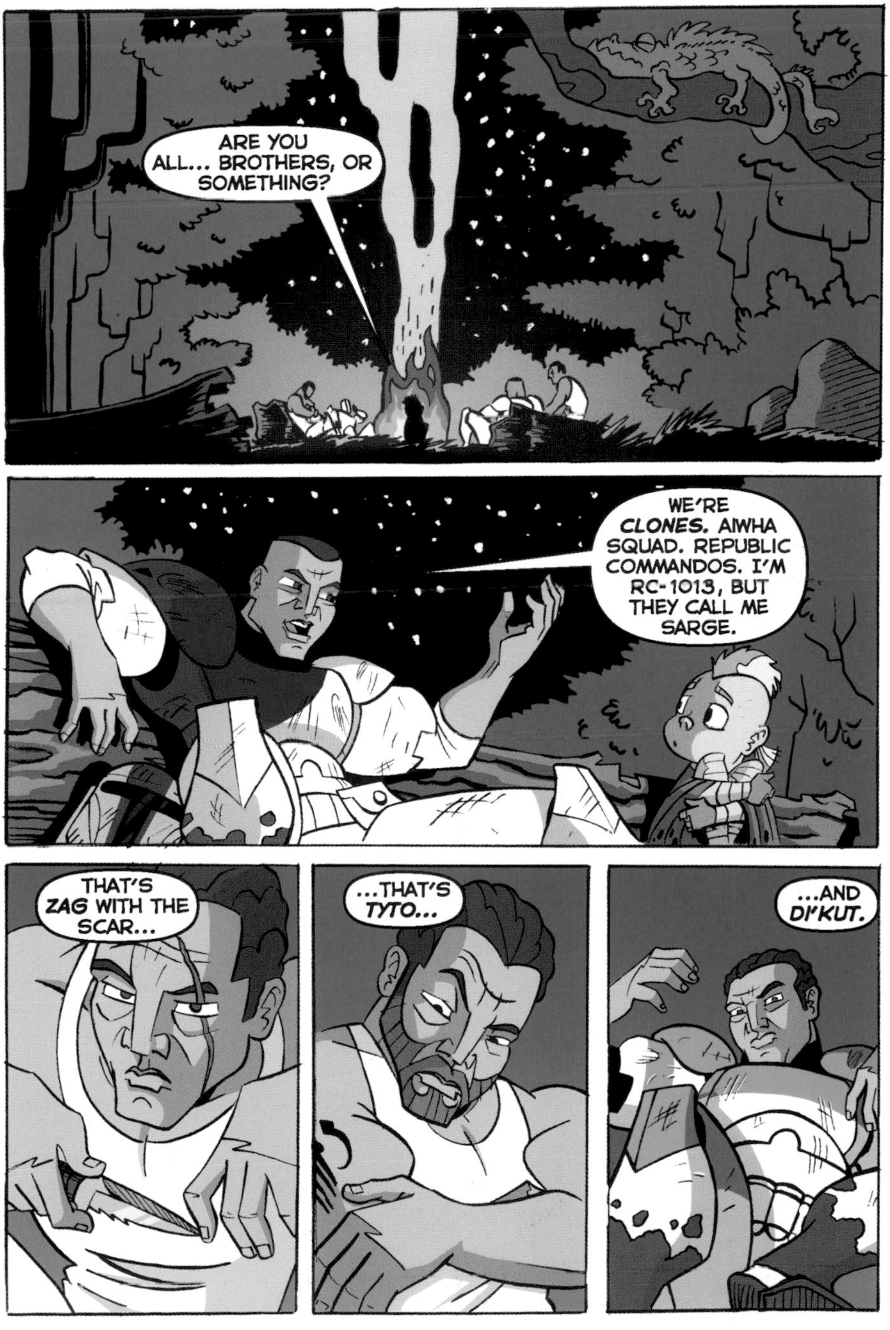
ARE YOU ALL... BROTHERS, OR SOMETHING?
WE'RE *CLONES.* AIWHA SQUAD. REPUBLIC COMMANDOS. I'M RC-1013, BUT THEY CALL ME SARGE.
THAT'S ZAG WITH THE SCAR...
...THAT'S *TYTO...*
...AND *DI'KUT.*

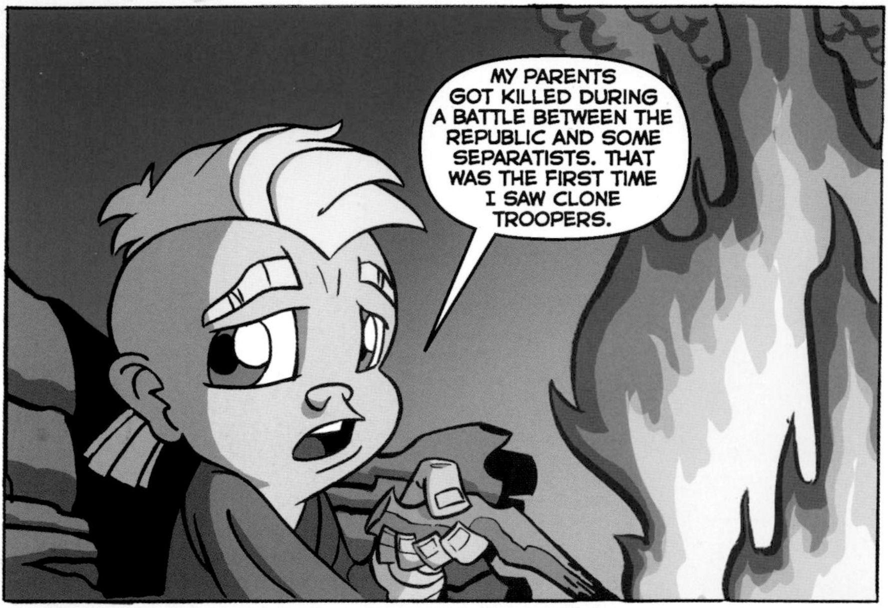
MY PARENTS GOT KILLED DURING A BATTLE BETWEEN THE REPUBLIC AND SOME SEPARATISTS. THAT WAS THE FIRST TIME I SAW CLONE TROOPERS.

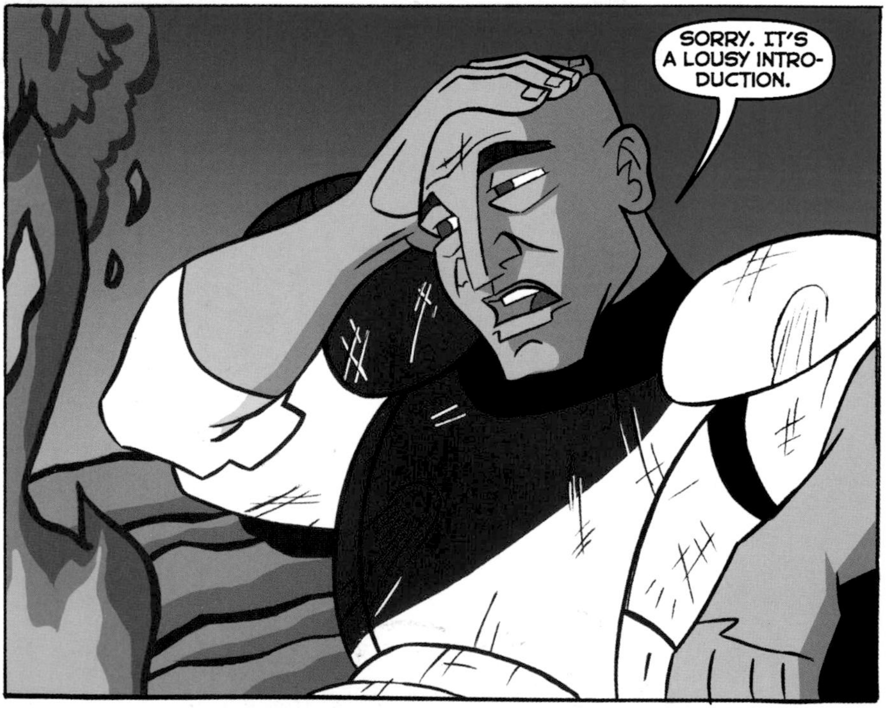
SORRY. IT'S A LOUSY INTRODUCTION.

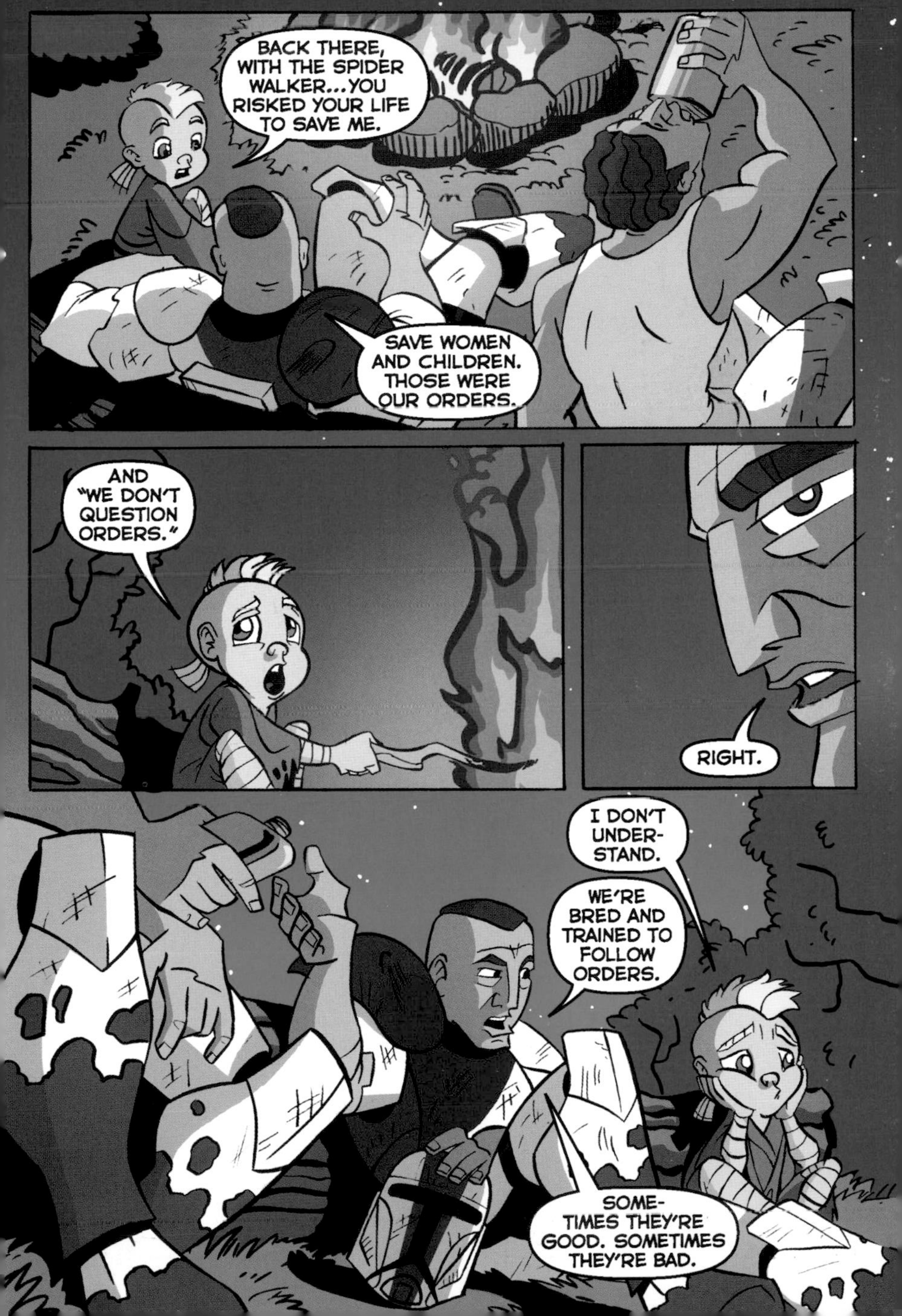
BACK THERE, WITH THE SPIDER WALKER...YOU RISKED YOUR LIFE TO SAVE ME.
SAVE WOMEN AND CHILDREN. THOSE WERE OUR ORDERS.
AND "WE DON'T QUESTION ORDERS."
RIGHT.
I DON'T UNDER-STAND.
WE'RE BRED AND TRAINED TO FOLLOW ORDERS.
SOME-TIMES THEY'RE GOOD. SOMETIMES THEY'RE BAD.

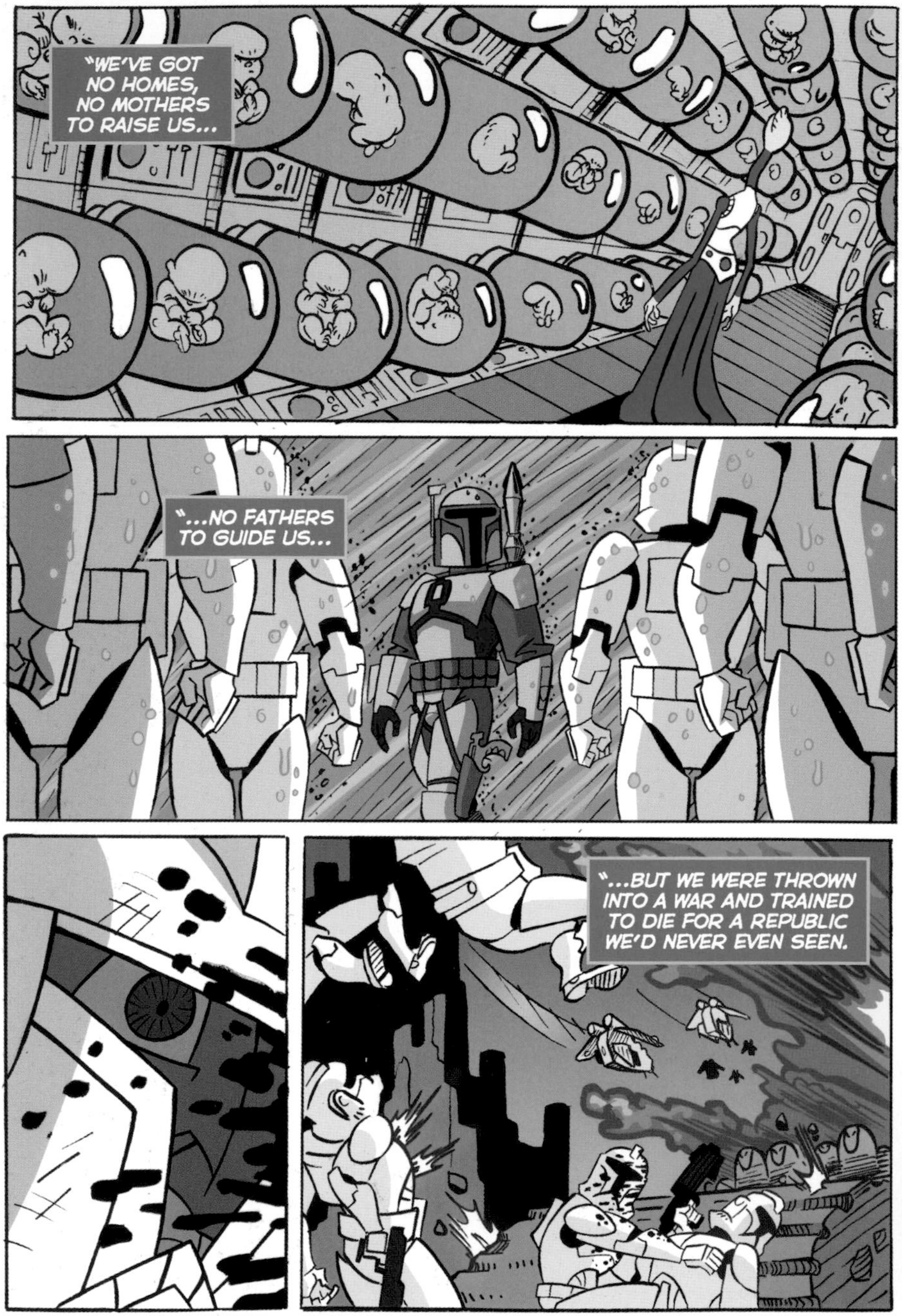
"WE'VE GOT NO HOMES, NO MOTHERS TO RAISE US...
"...NO FATHERS TO GUIDE US...
"...BUT WE WERE THROWN INTO A WAR AND TRAINED TO DIE FOR A REPUBLIC WE'D NEVER EVEN SEEN.

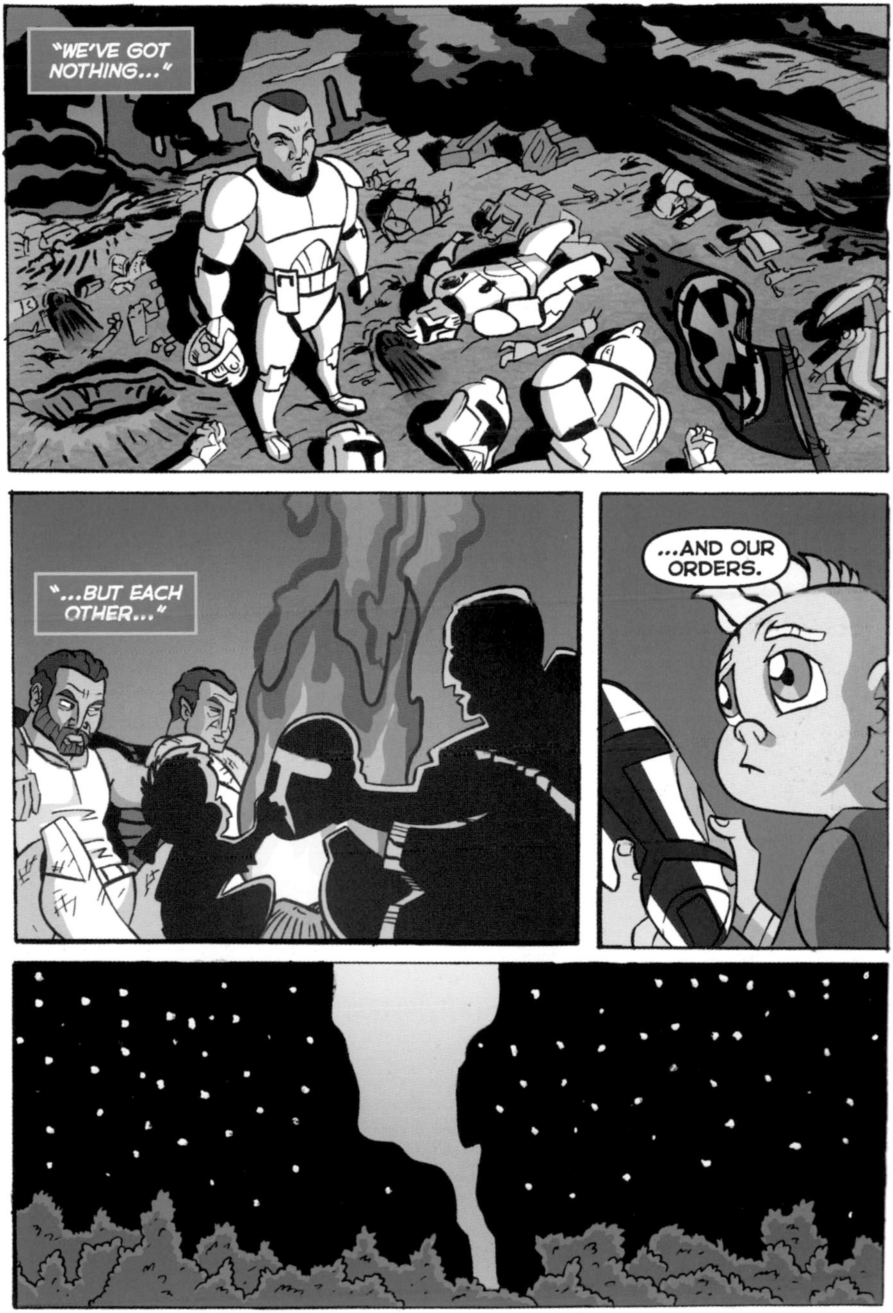
"WE'VE GOT NOTHING..."
"...BUT EACH OTHER..."
...AND OUR ORDERS.

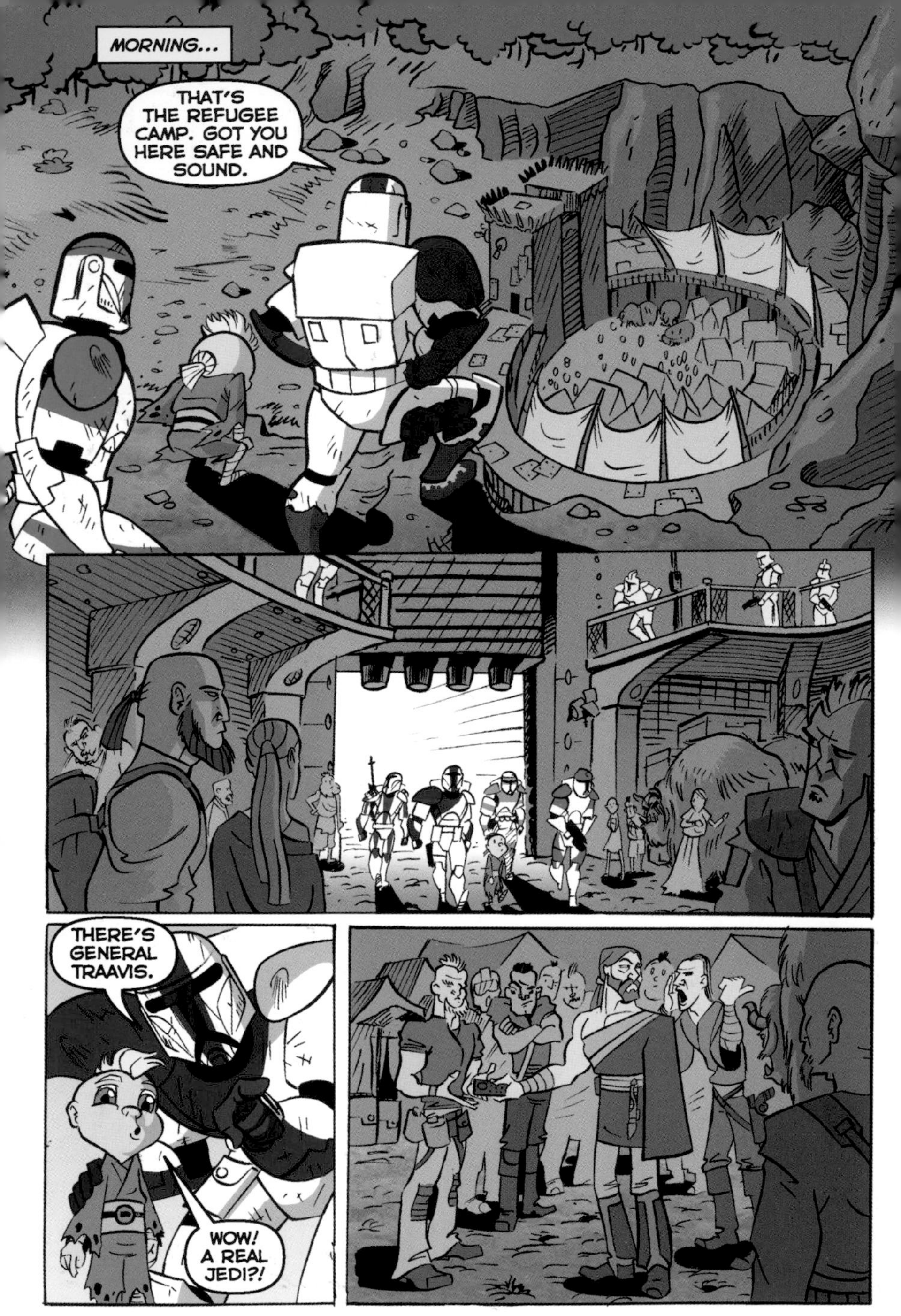
MORNING...
THAT'S THE REFUGEE CAMP. GOT YOU HERE SAFE AND SOUND.
THERE'S GENERAL TRAAVIS.
WOW! A REAL JEDI?!

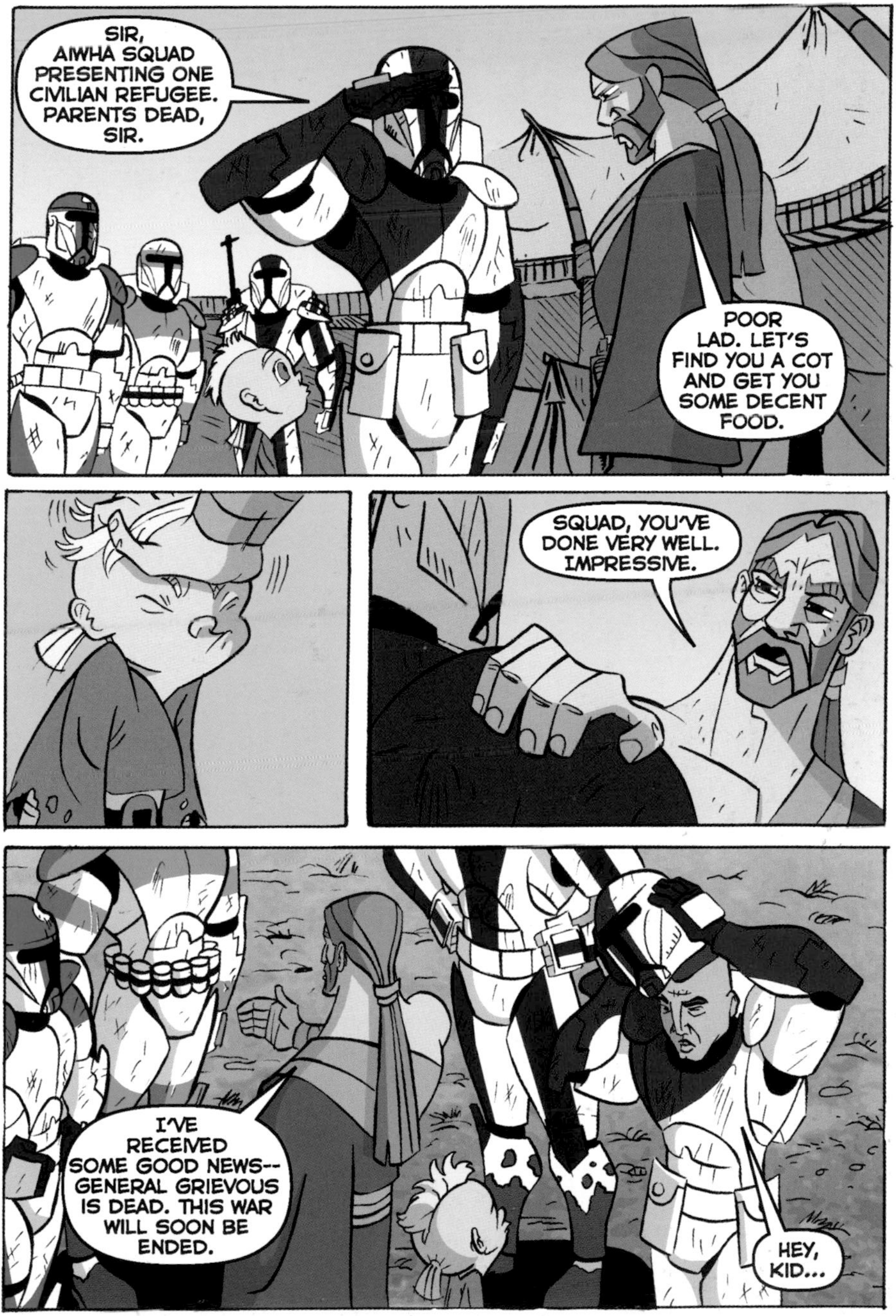
SIR, AIWHA SQUAD PRESENTING ONE CIVILIAN REFUGEE. PARENTS DEAD, SIR.
POOR LAD. LET'S FIND YOU A COT AND GET YOU SOME DECENT FOOD.
SQUAD, YOU'VE DONE VERY WELL. IMPRESSIVE.
I'VE RECEIVED SOME GOOD NEWS-- GENERAL GRIEVOUS IS DEAD. THIS WAR WILL SOON BE ENDED.
HEY, KID...

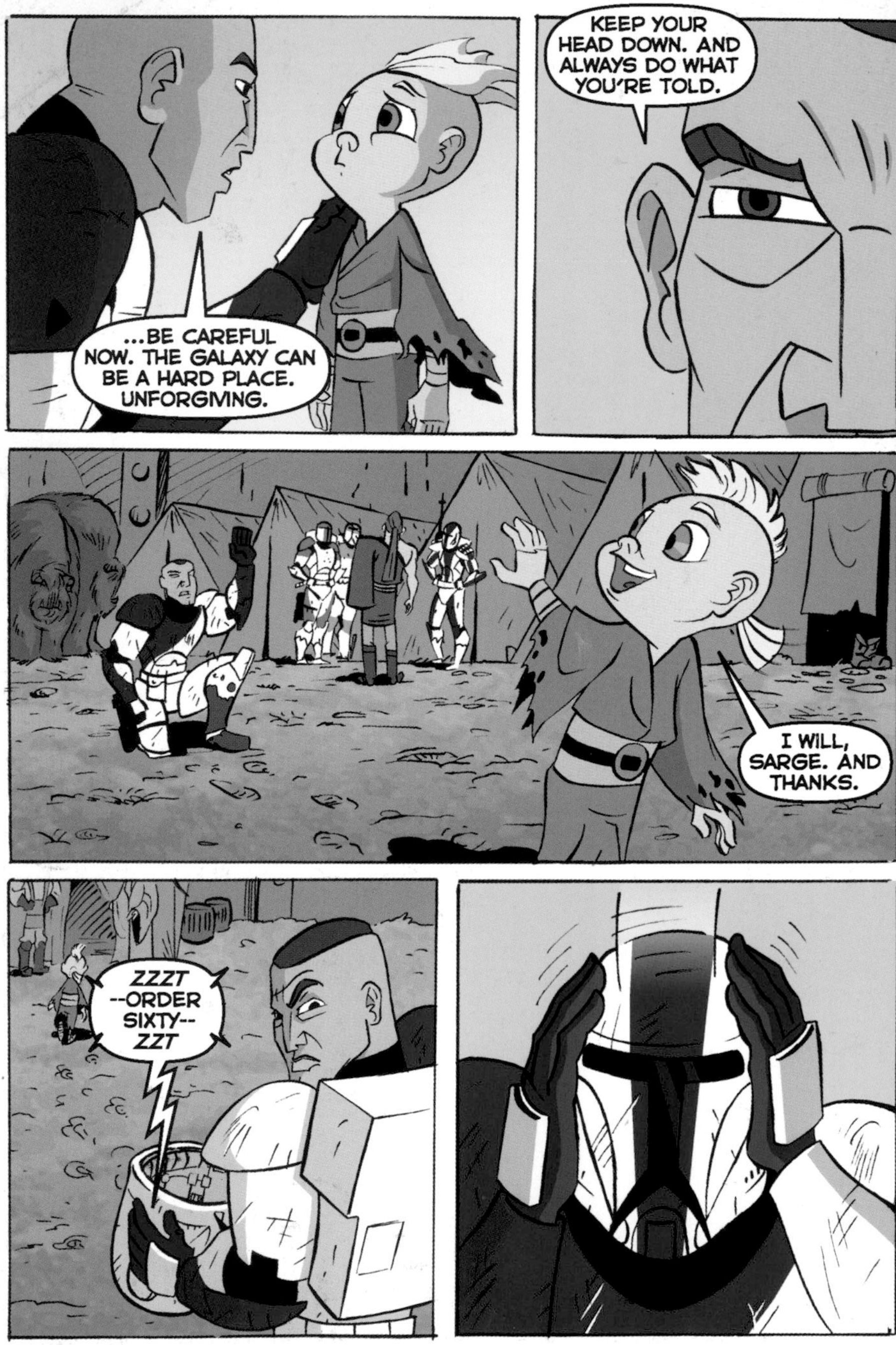
...BE CAREFUL NOW. THE GALAXY CAN BE A HARD PLACE. UNFORGIVING.
KEEP YOUR HEAD DOWN. AND ALWAYS DO WHAT YOU'RE TOLD.
I WILL, SARGE. AND THANKS.
ZZZT --ORDER SIXTY-- ZZT

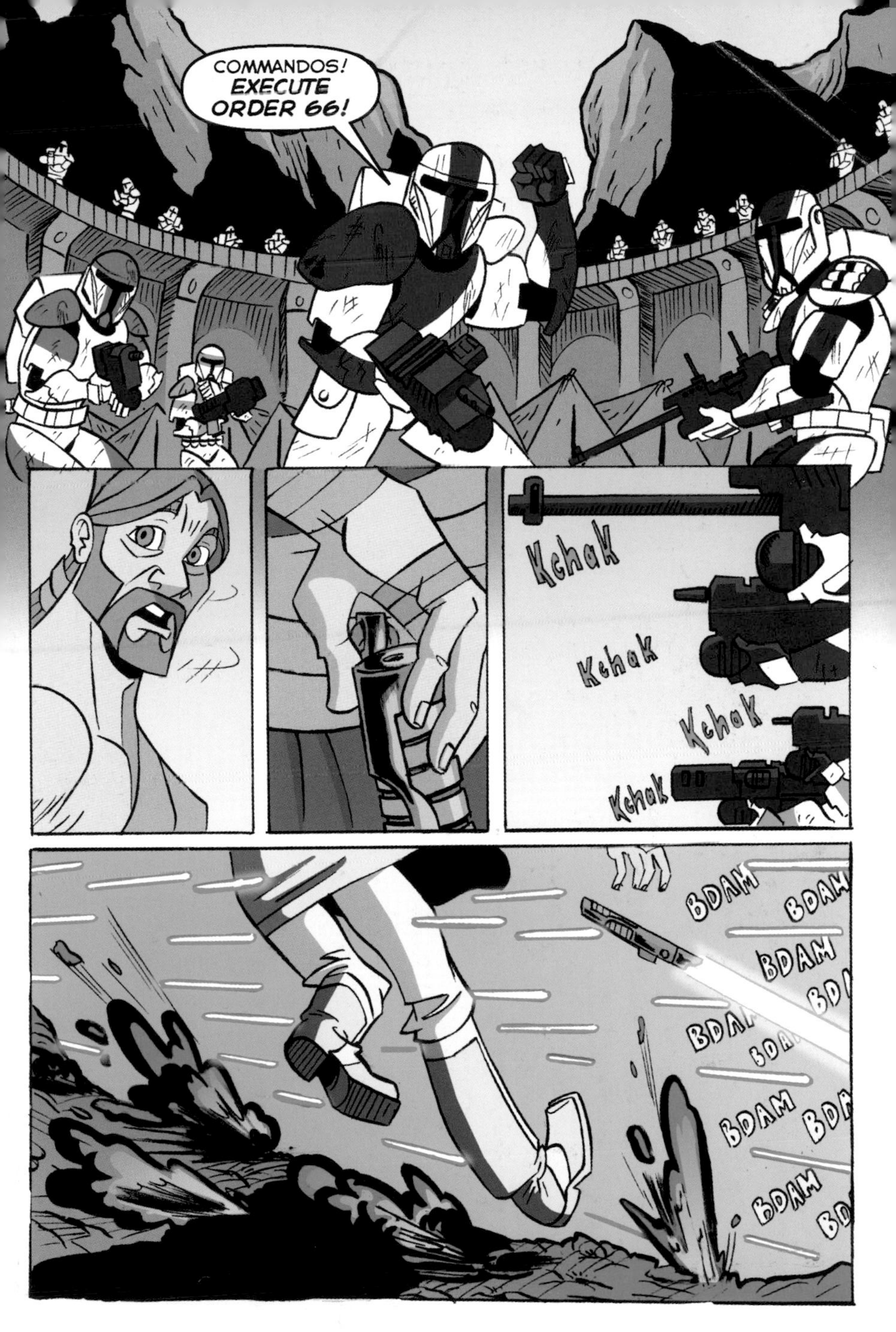
COMMANDOS! EXECUTE ORDER 66!
Kchak
Kchak
Kchak
Kchak
BDAM
BDAM
BDAM
BDAM
BDAM
BDAM
BDAM

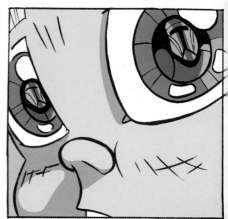

THE JEDI WERE TRAITORS TO THE REPUBLIC. WE FOLLOWED OUR ORDERS.

AND WE DON'T QUESTION ORDERS...

THE END

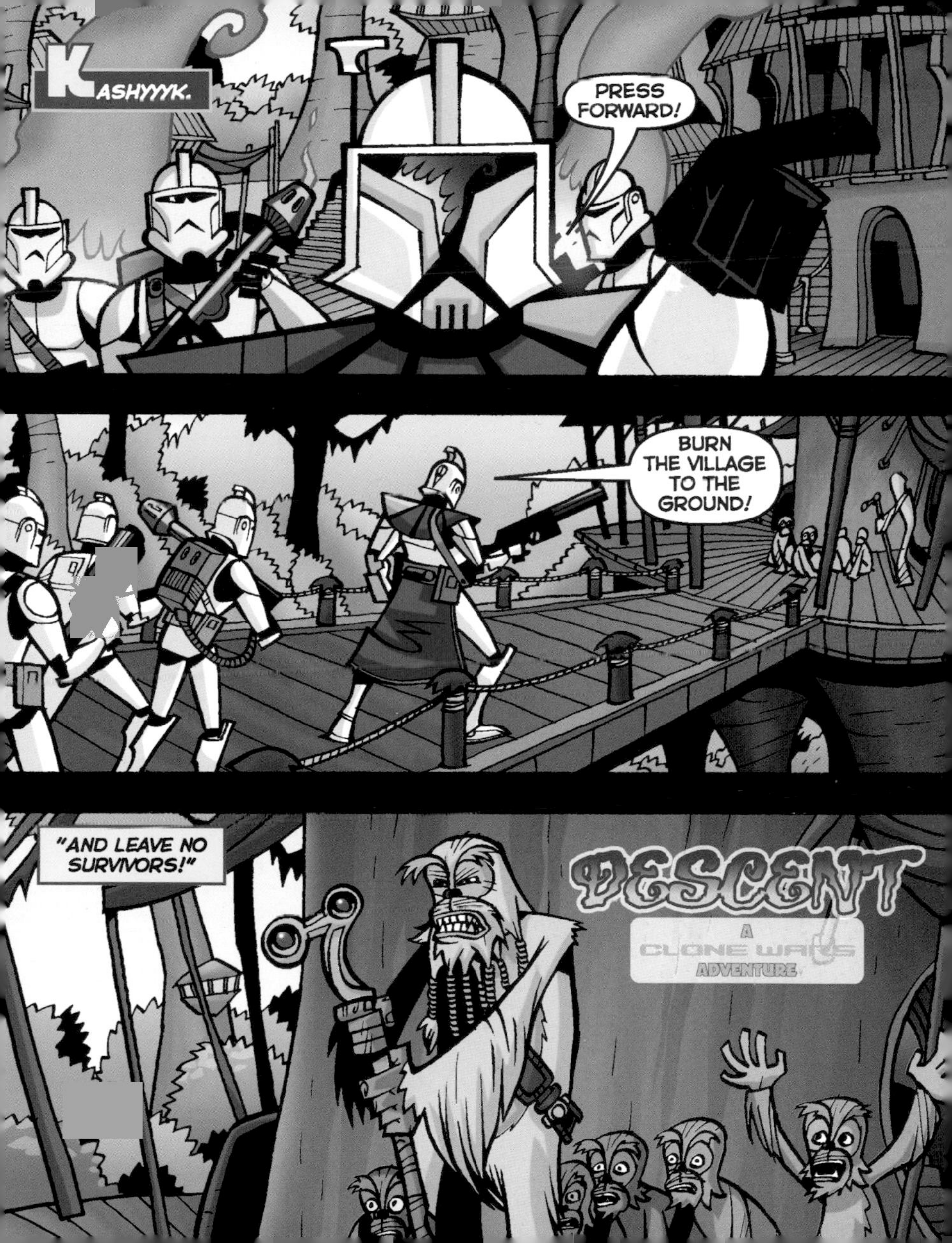
KASHYYYK.
PRESS FORWARD!
BURN THE VILLAGE TO THE GROUND!
"AND LEAVE NO SURVIVORS!"
DESCENT
A CLONE WARS ADVENTURE

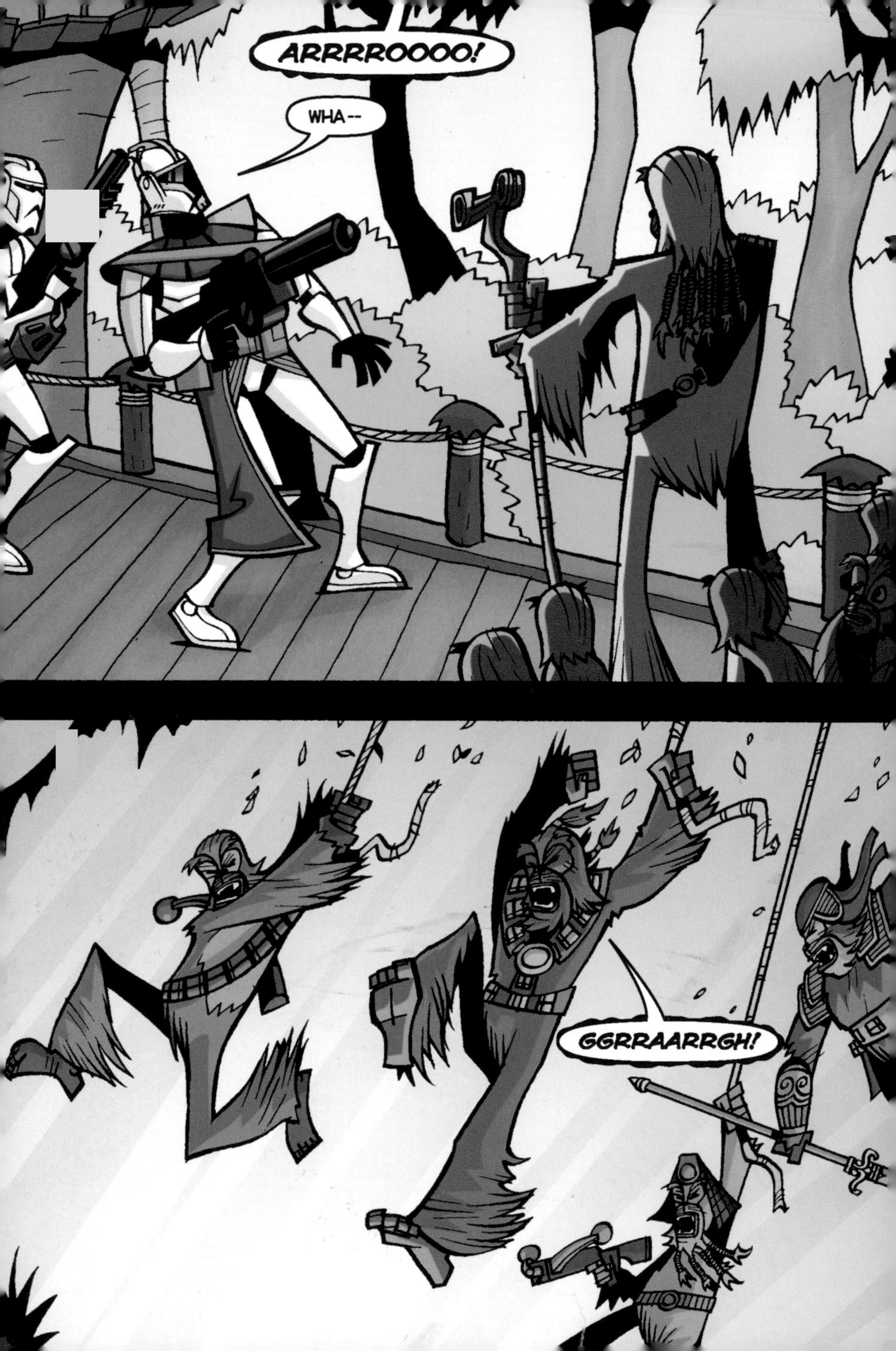
ARRRROOOO!
WHA--
GGRRAARRGH!

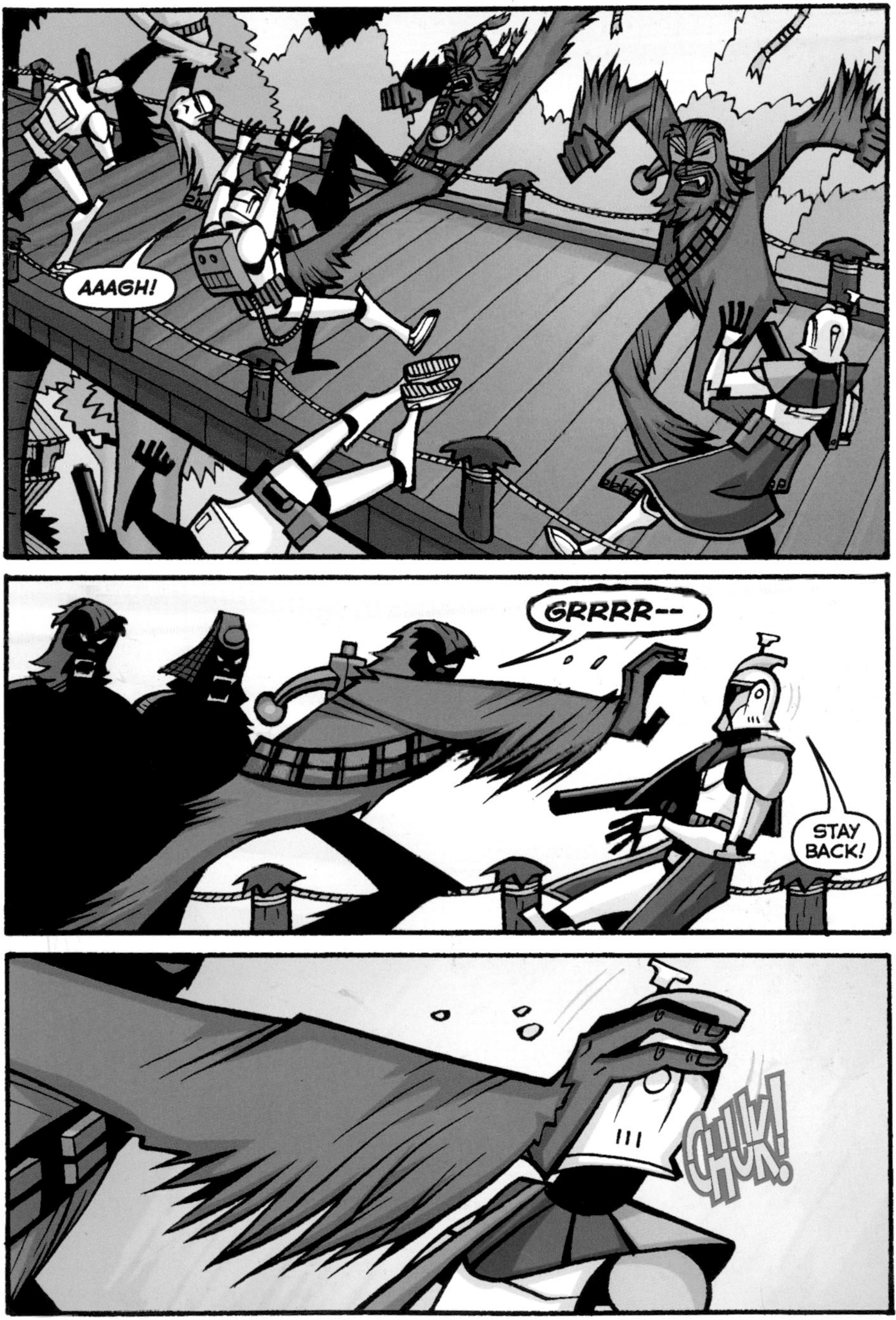
AAAGH!
GRRRR--
STAY BACK!
CHUK!

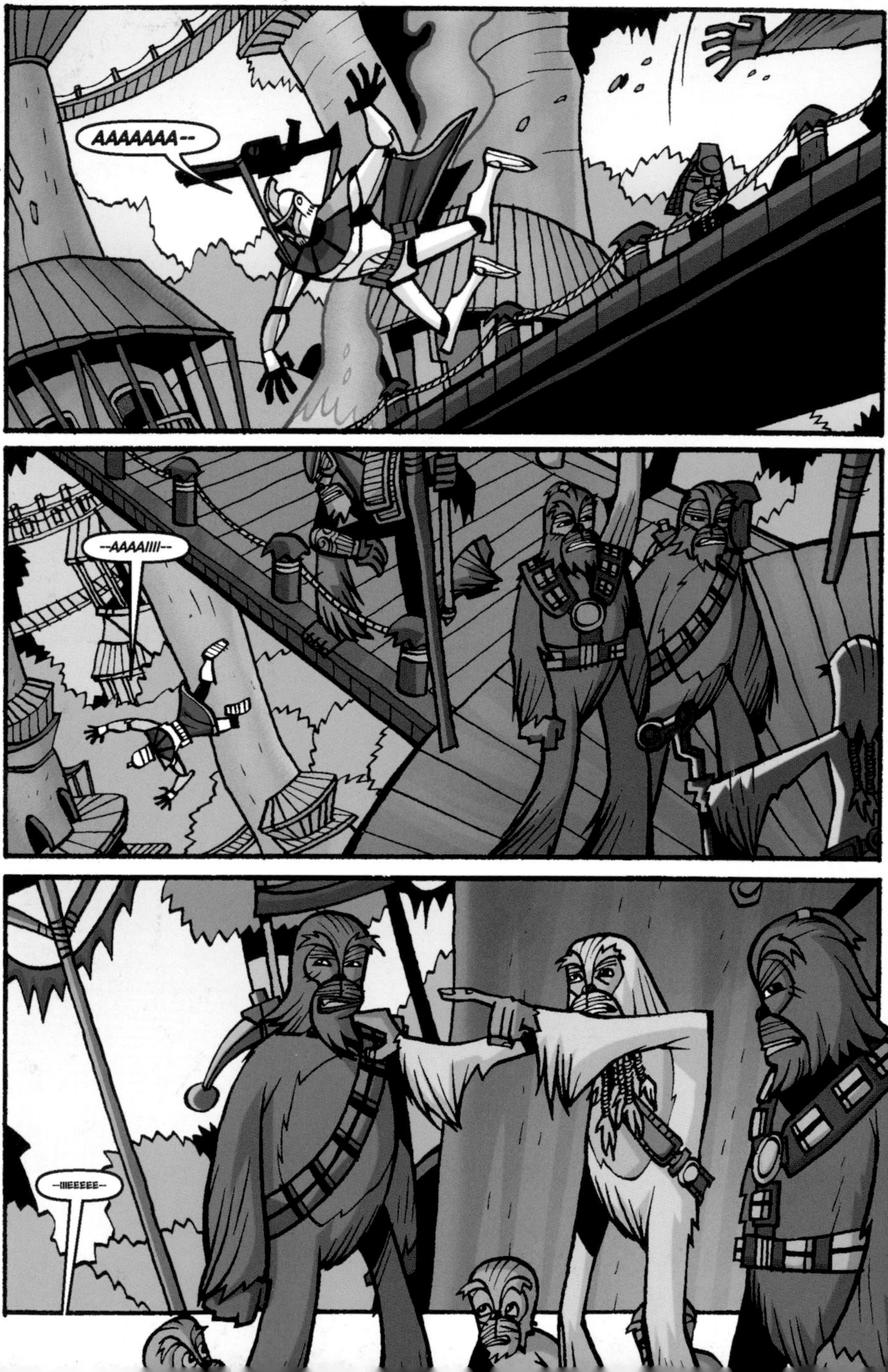
AAAAAAA--
--AAAAIIII--
--IIIEEEEE--

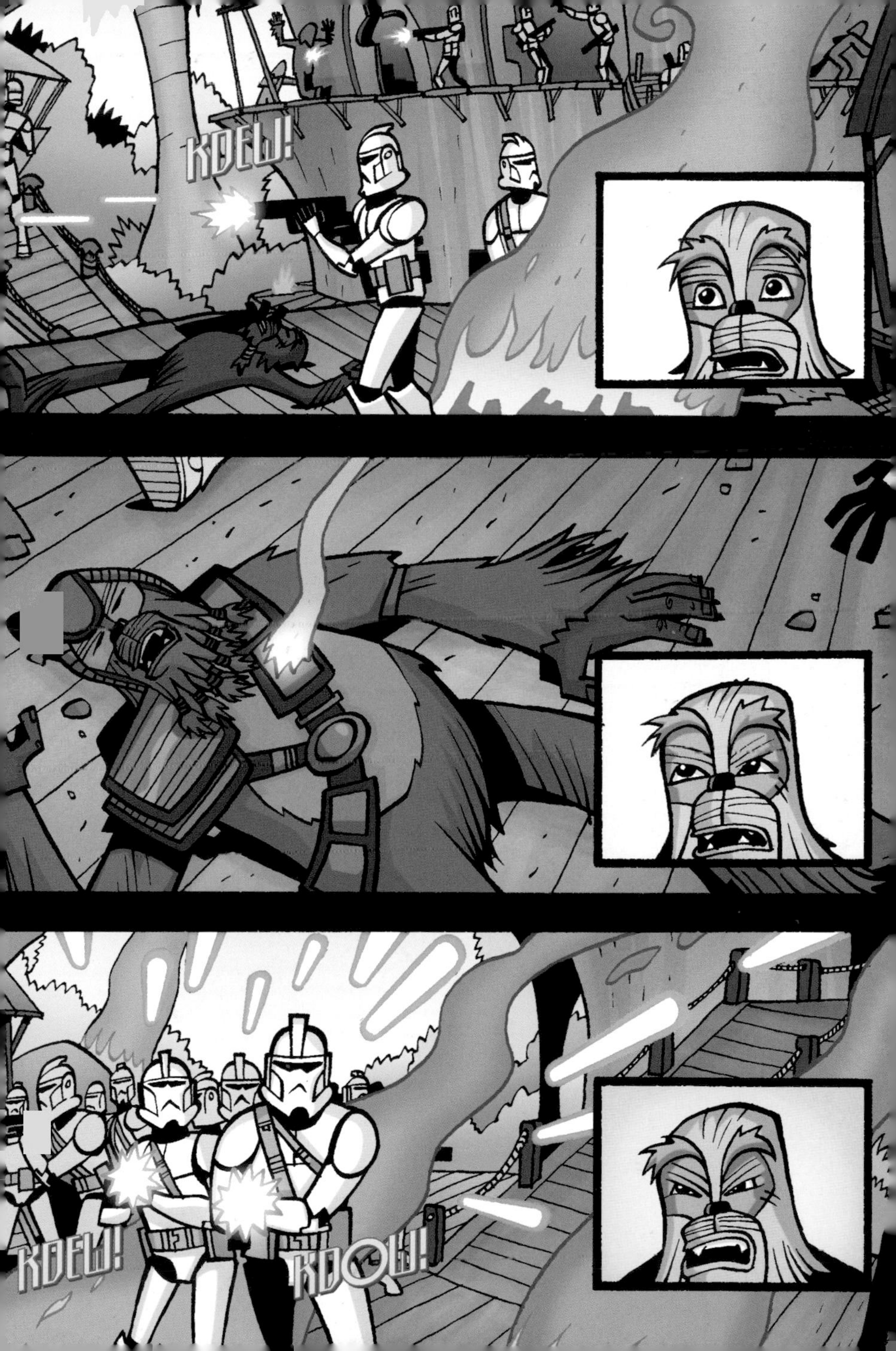
KDEW!
KDEW!
KDOW!

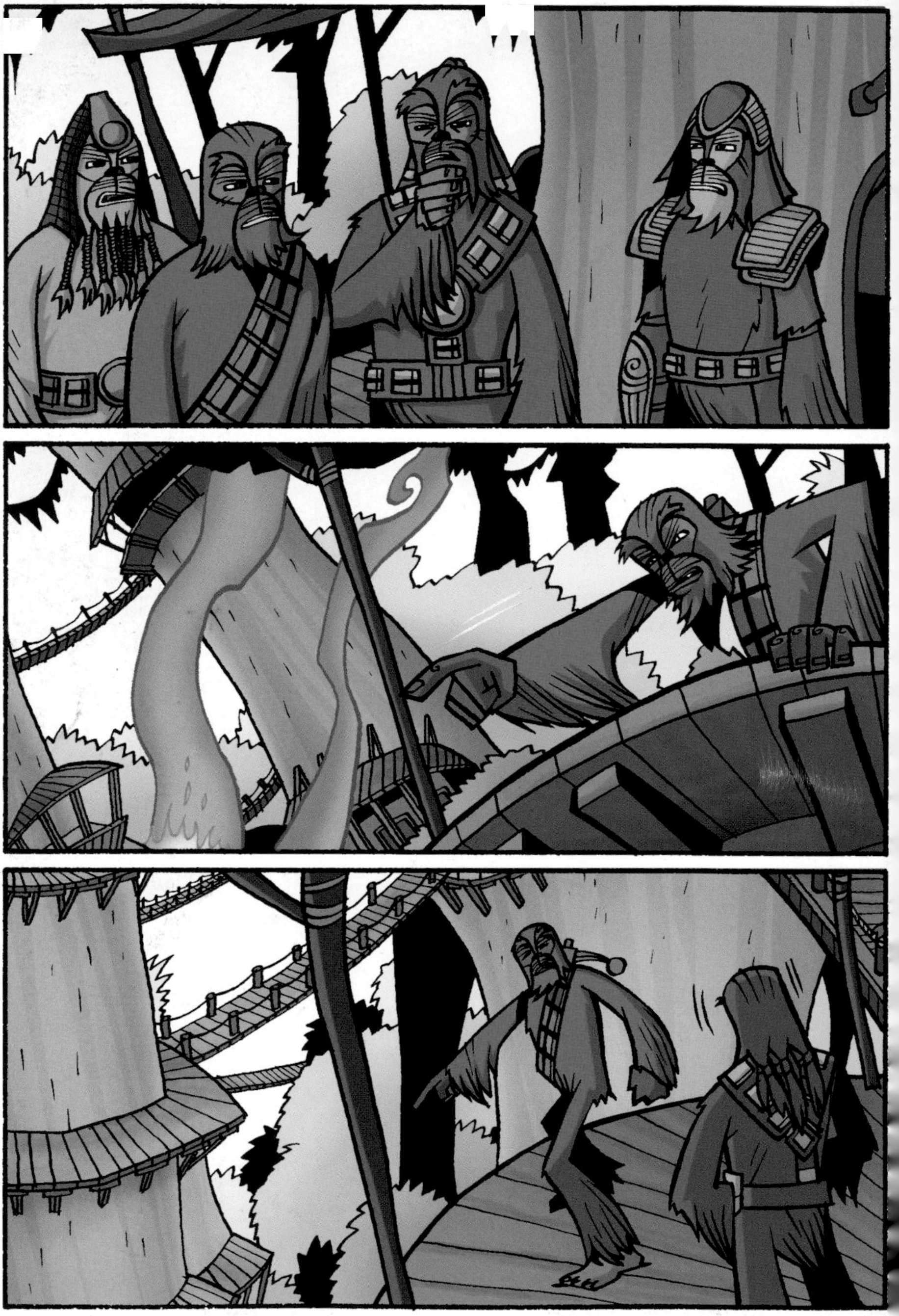

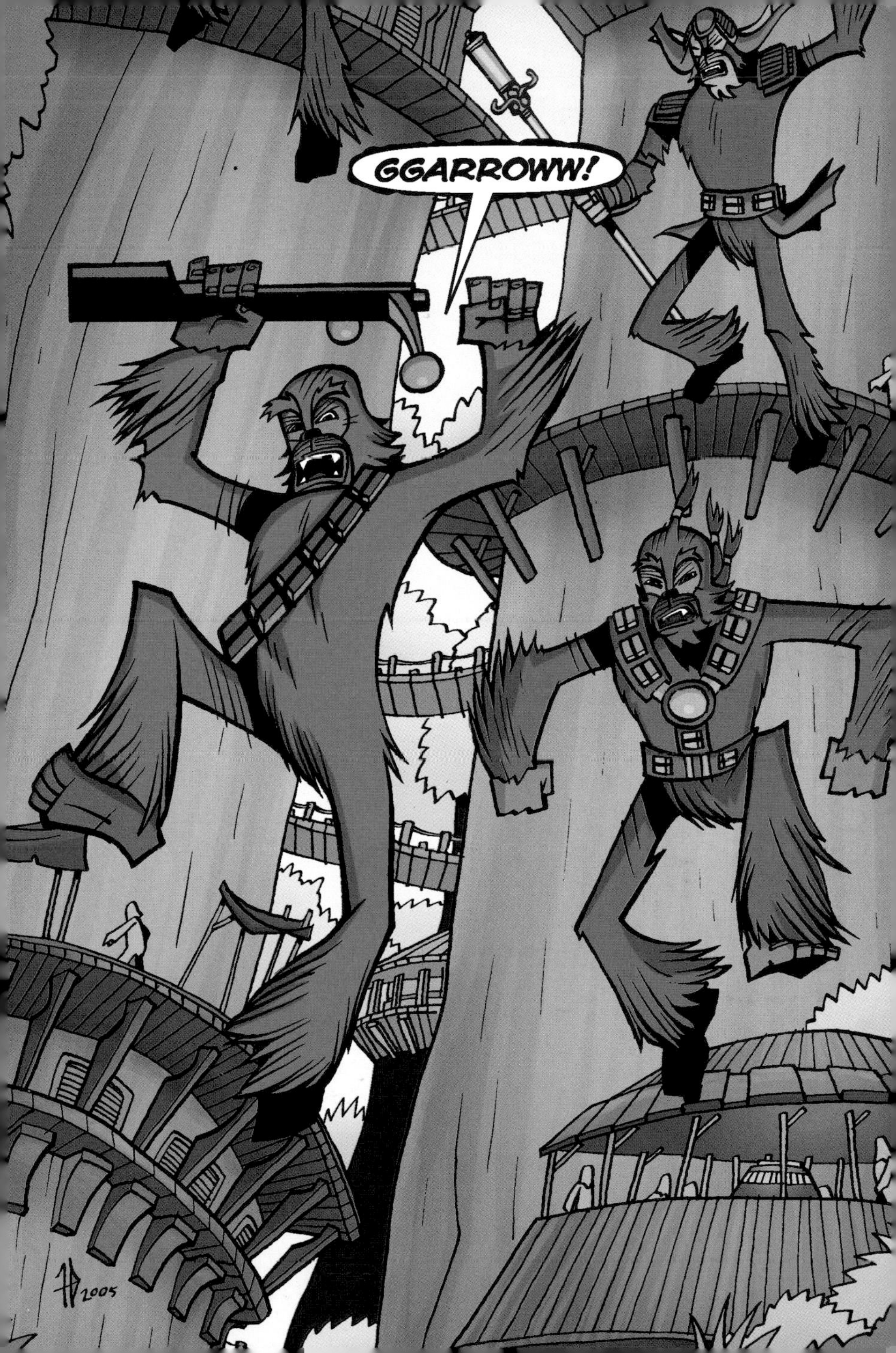
GGARROWW!
2005

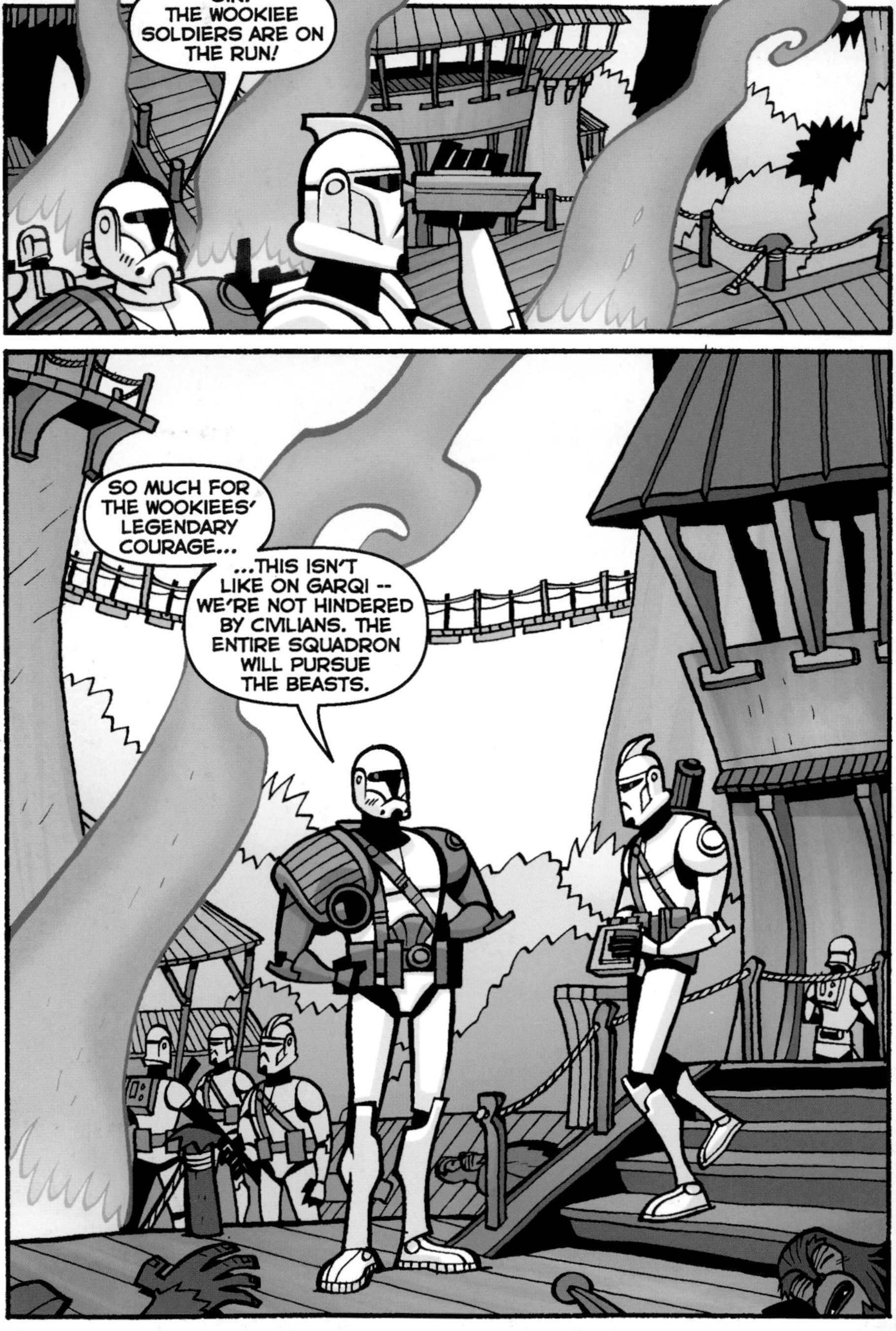
SIR! THE WOOKIEE SOLDIERS ARE ON THE RUN!
SO MUCH FOR THE WOOKIEES' LEGENDARY COURAGE...
...THIS ISN'T LIKE ON GARQI -- WE'RE NOT HINDERED BY CIVILIANS. THE ENTIRE SQUADRON WILL PURSUE THE BEASTS.

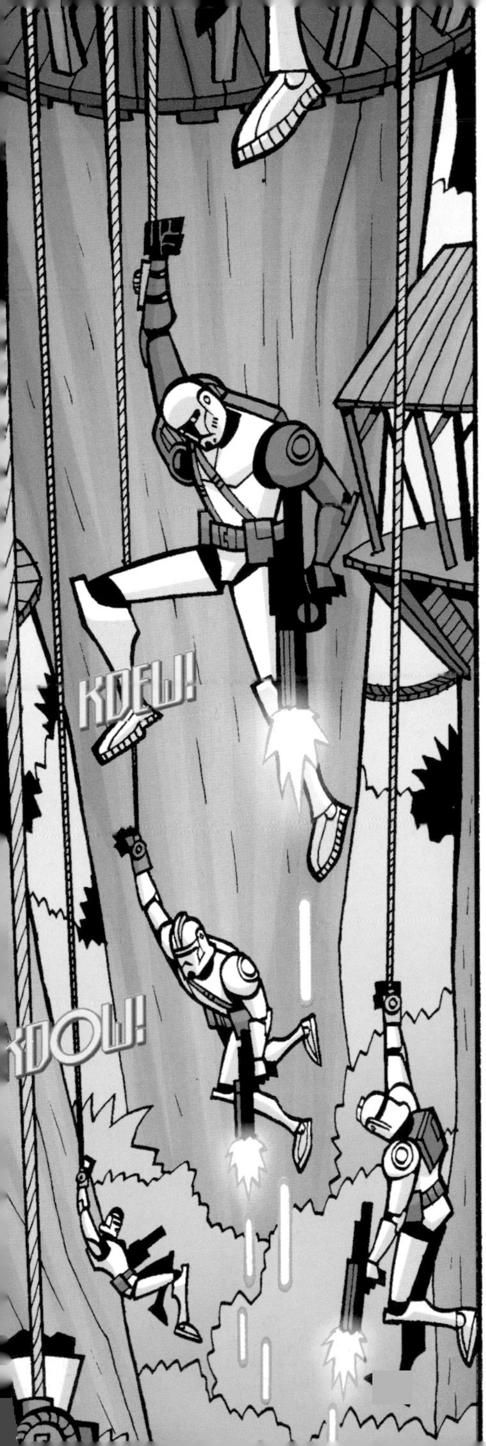
KDEW!

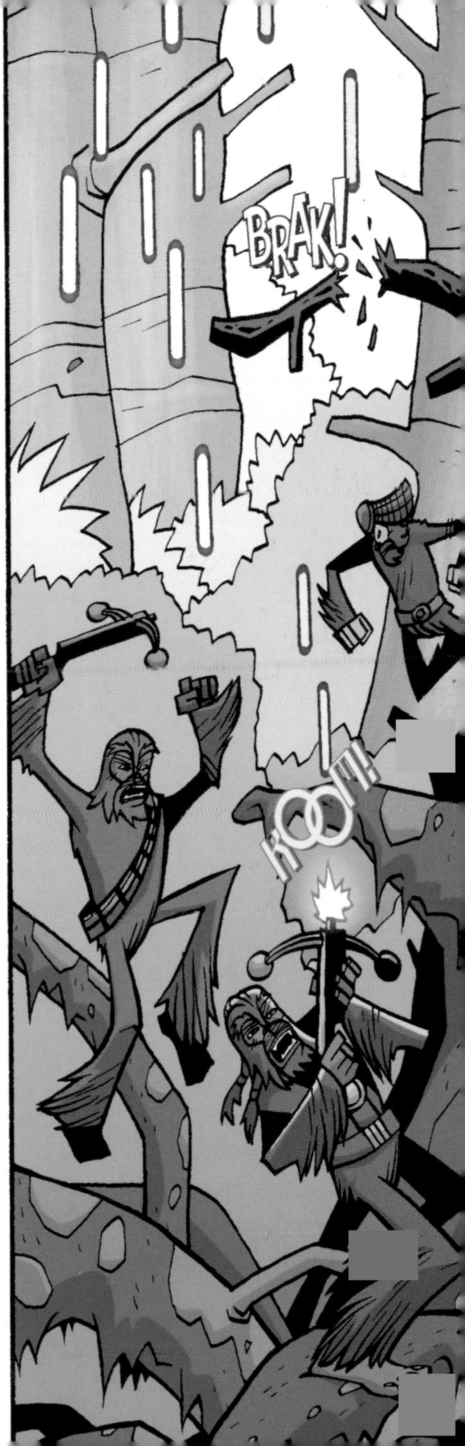
BRAK!
KOOM!

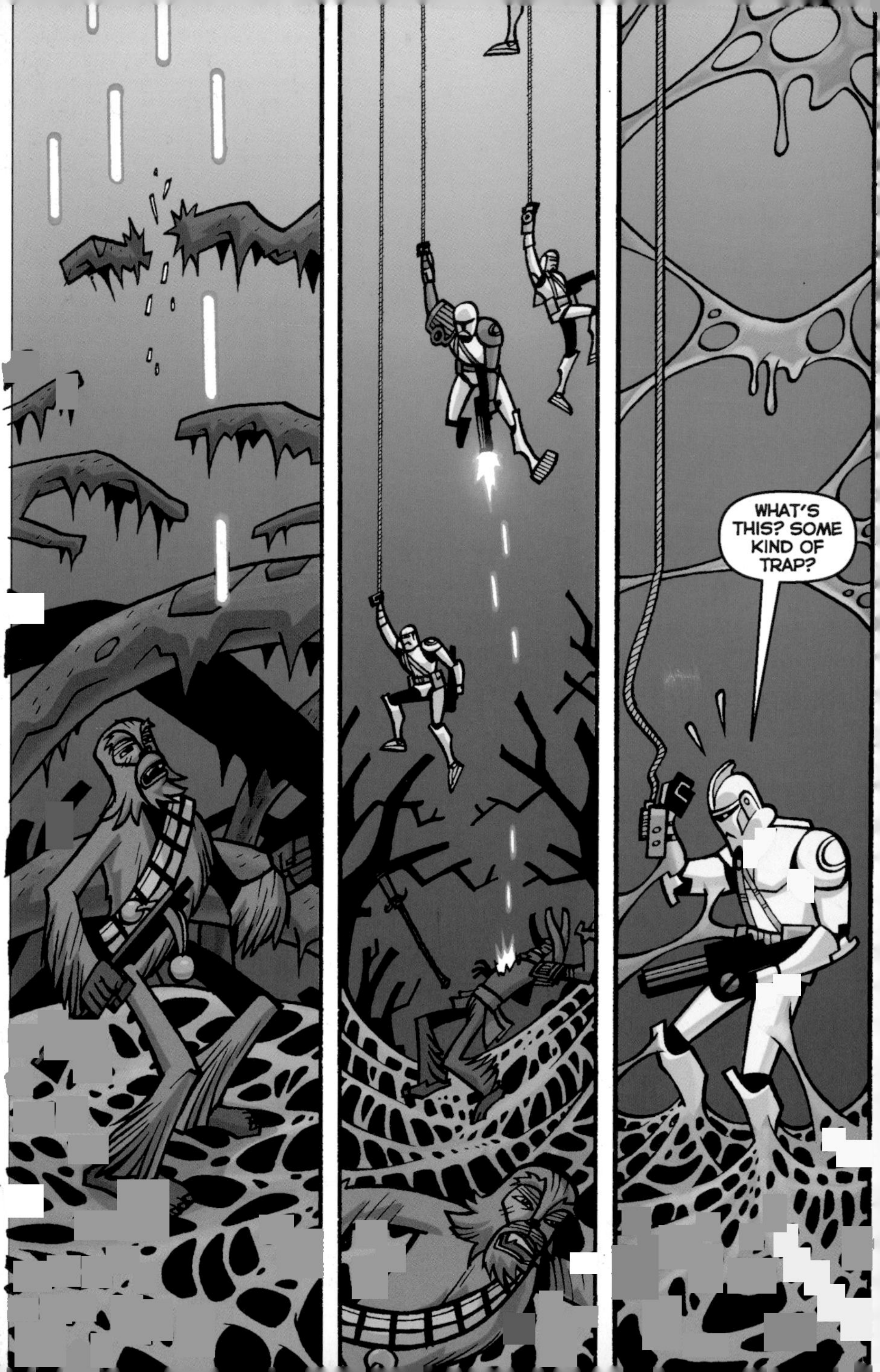
WHAT'S THIS? SOME KIND OF TRAP?

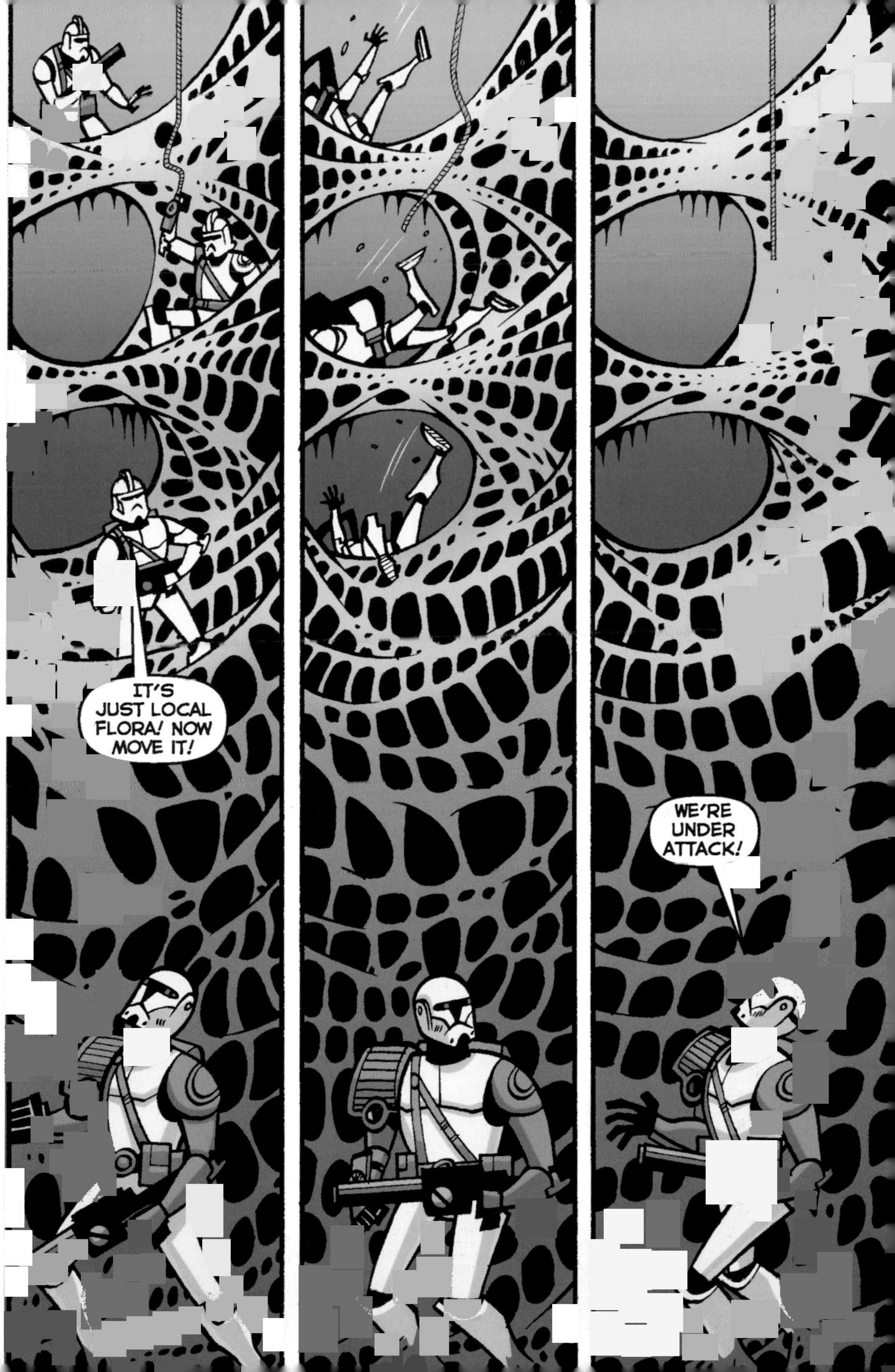
IT'S JUST LOCAL FLORA! NOW MOVE IT!
WE'RE UNDER ATTACK!

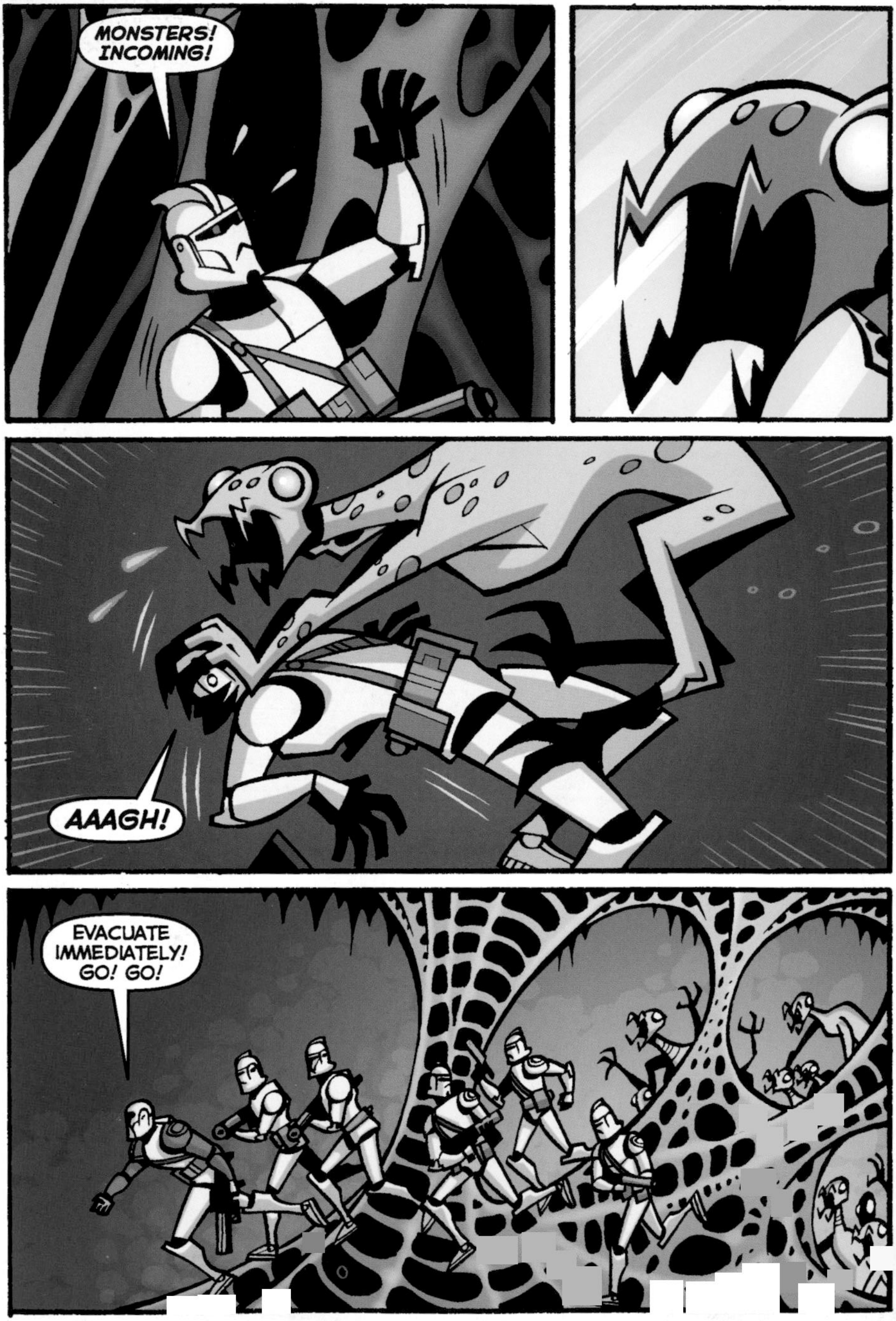
MONSTERS! INCOMING!
AAAGH!
EVACUATE IMMEDIATELY! GO! GO!

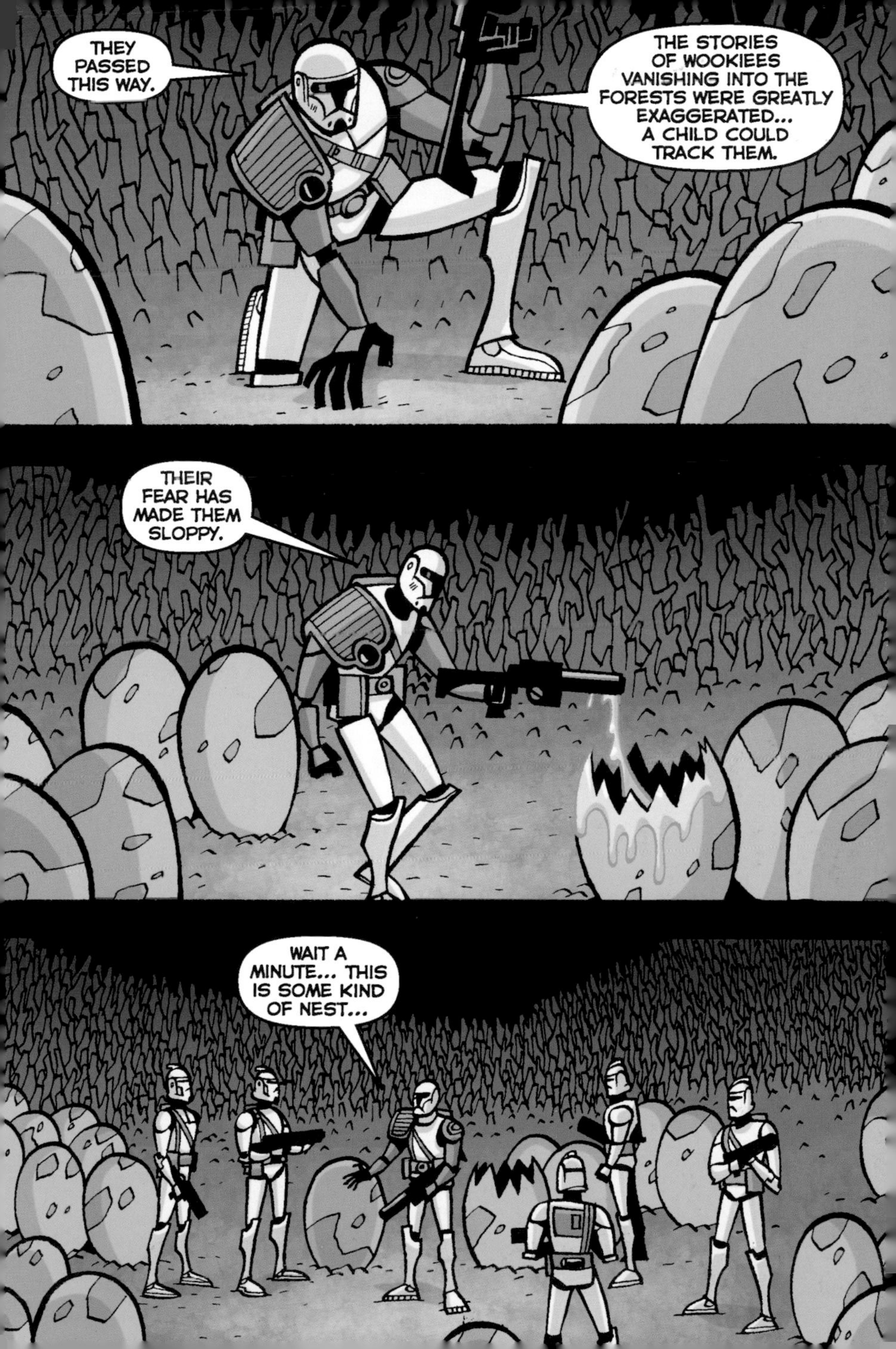
THEY PASSED THIS WAY.
THE STORIES OF WOOKIEES VANISHING INTO THE FORESTS WERE GREATLY EXAGGERATED... A CHILD COULD TRACK THEM.
THEIR FEAR HAS MADE THEM SLOPPY.
WAIT A MINUTE... THIS IS SOME KIND OF NEST...

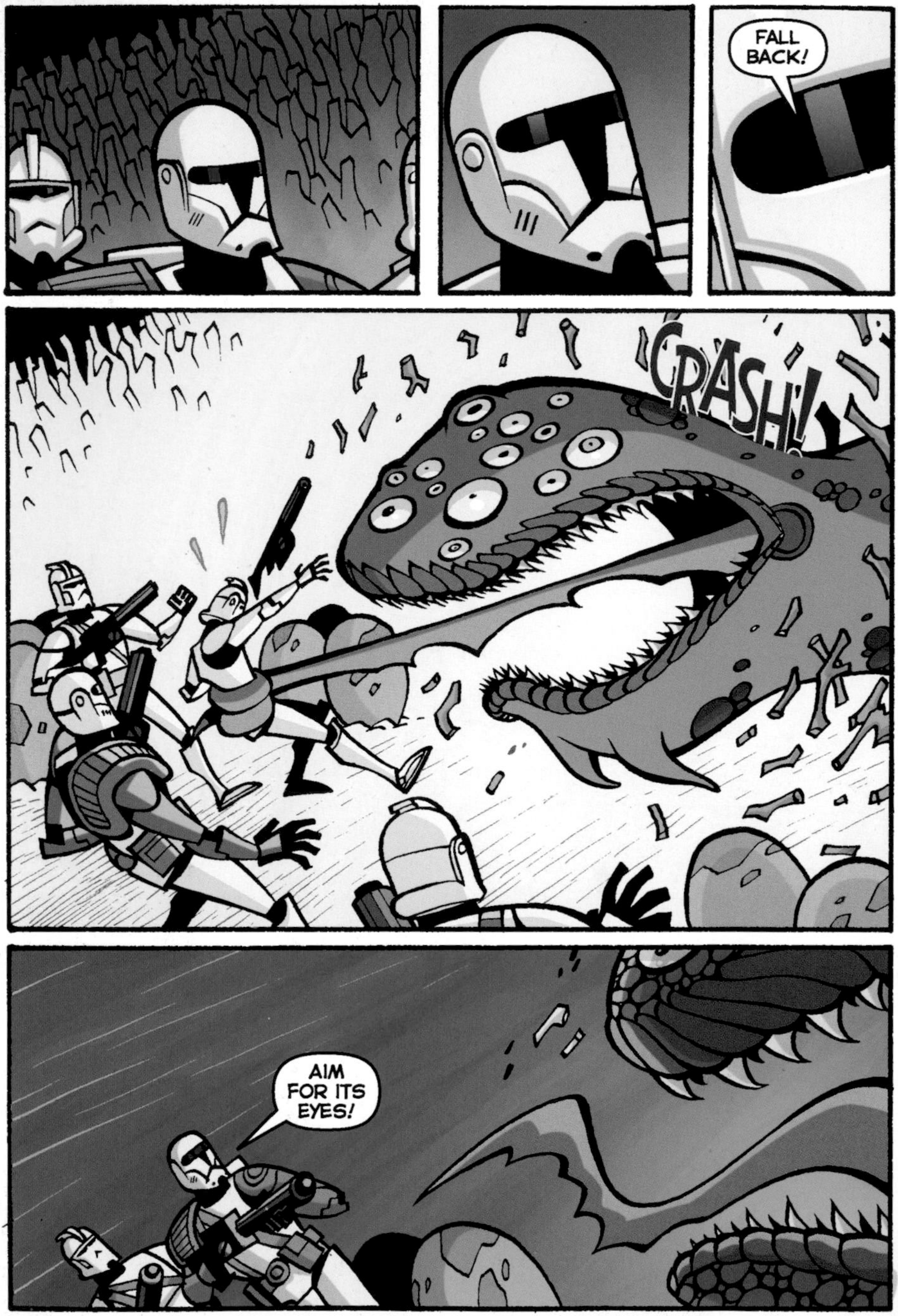
FALL BACK!
CRASH!
AIM FOR ITS EYES!

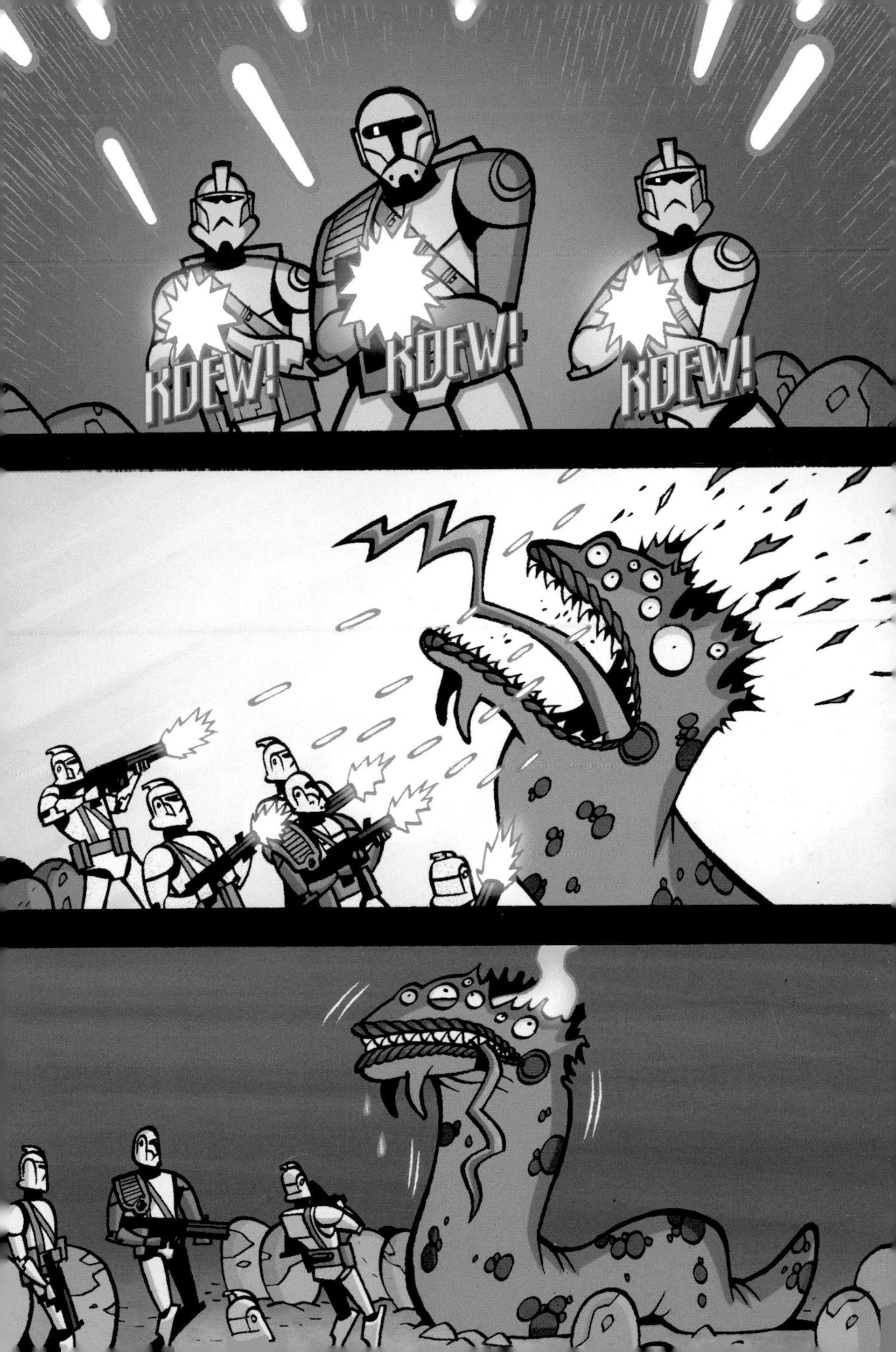
KDEW!
KDEW!
KDEW!

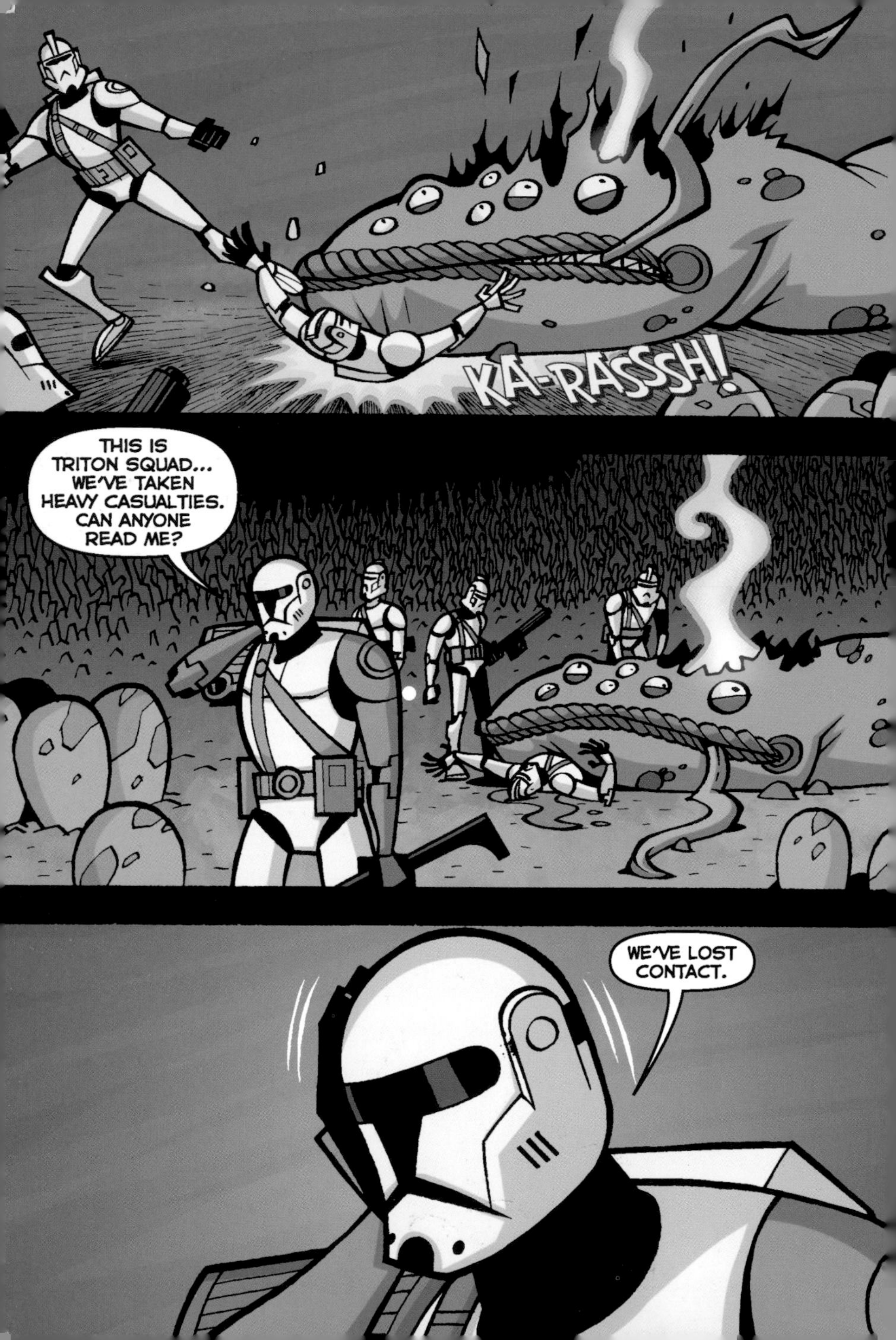
KA-RASSSH!
THIS IS TRITON SQUAD... WE'VE TAKEN HEAVY CASUALTIES. CAN ANYONE READ ME?
WE'VE LOST CONTACT.

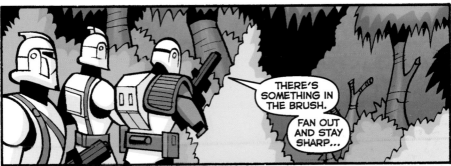

THERE'S SOMETHING IN THE BRUSH.

FAN OUT AND STAY SHARP...

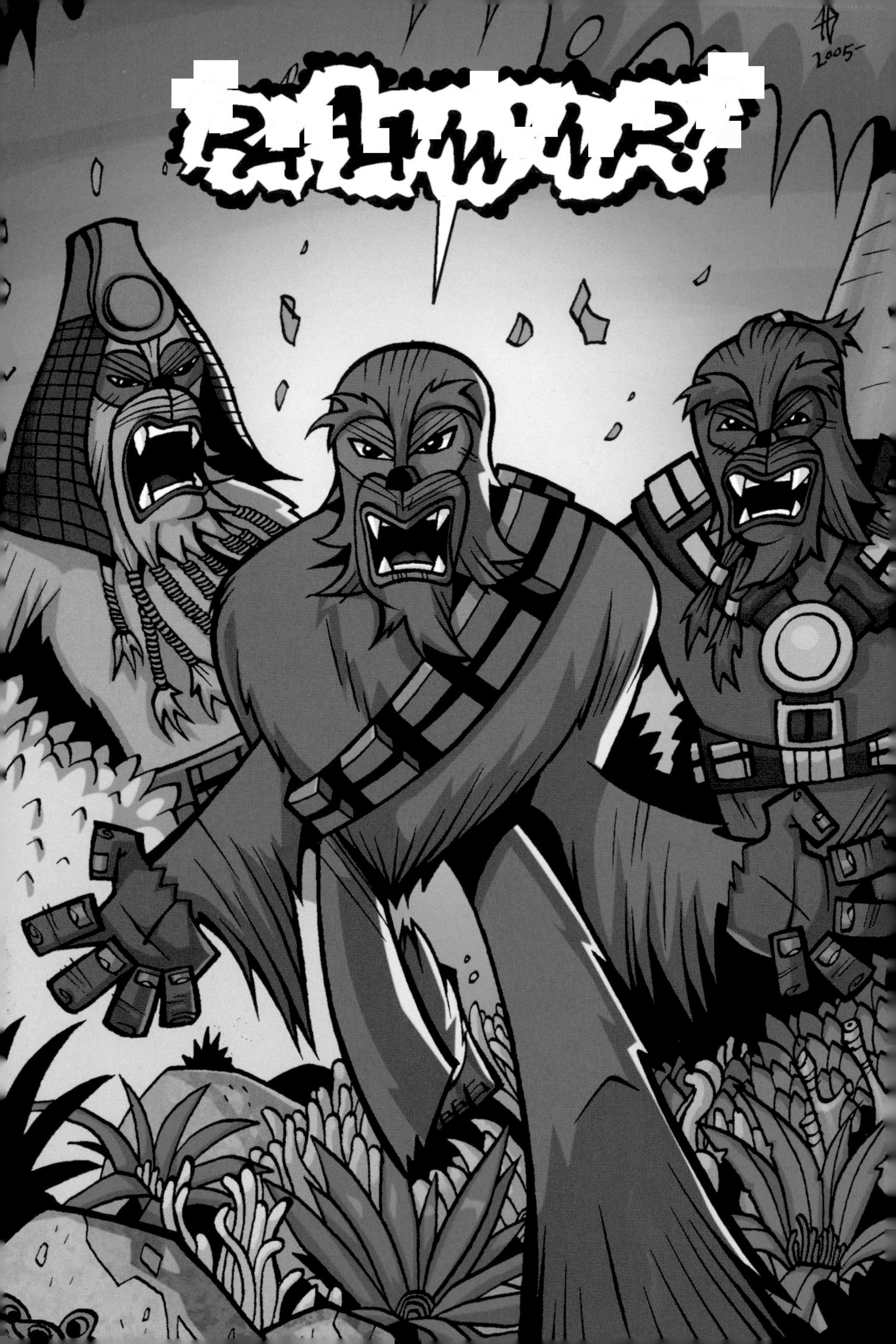

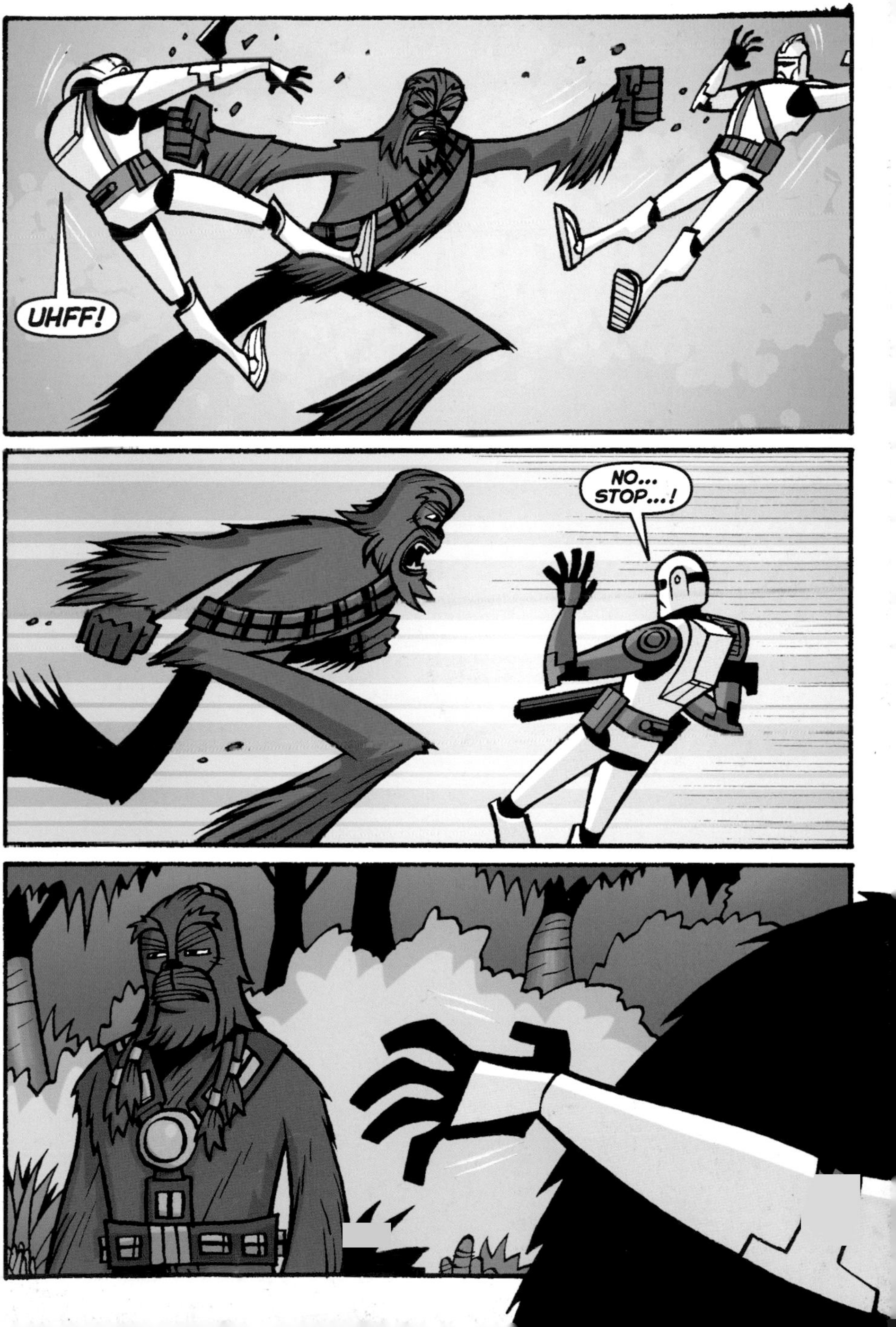
UHFF!
NO... STOP...!

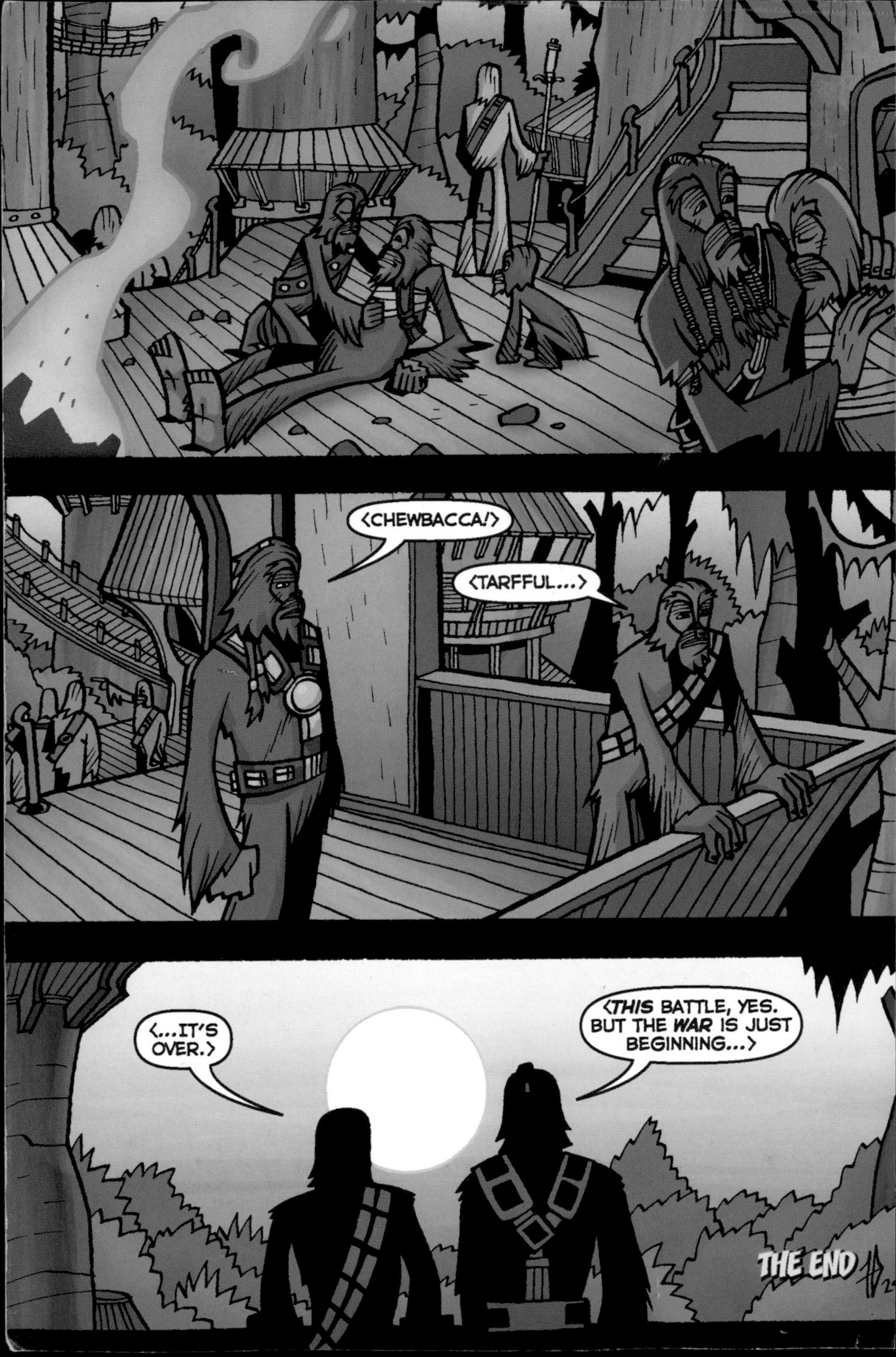
<CHEWBACCA!>
<TARFFUL...>
<...IT'S OVER.>
<THIS BATTLE, YES. BUT THE WAR IS JUST BEGINNING...>
THE END

Don't miss any of the action-packed adventures of your favorite **STAR WARS**®
characters, availble at comics shops and bookstores in a galaxy near you!

Volume 1
ISBN: 1-59307-243-0 / $6.95

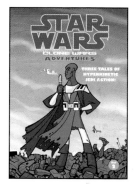

Volume 2
ISBN: 1-59307-271-6 / $6.95

Volume 3
ISBN: 1-59307-307-0 / $6.95

Volume 4
ISBN: 1-59307-402-6 / $6.95

CLONE WARS

Experience all the excitement and drama of the Clone Wars! Look for these trade paperbacks at a comics shop or book store near you!

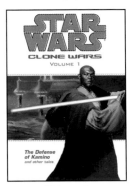

Volume 1
ISBN: 1-56971-962-4 / $14.95

Volume 2
ISBN: 1-56971-969-1 / $14.95

Volume 3
ISBN: 1-59307-006-3 / $14.95

Volume 4
ISBN: 1-59307-195-7 / $16.95

ALSO AVAILABLE

Volume 5
ISBN: 1-59307-273-2 / $14.95

Volume 6
ISBN: 1-59307-352-6 / $17.95

To find a comics shop in your area, call 1-888-266-4226
For more information or to order direct: • On the web: darkhorse.com • E-mail: mailorder@darkhorse.com
• Phone: 1-800-862-0052 or (503) 652-9701 Mon.-Sat. 9 A.M. to 5 P.M. Pacific Time